The Practical to Revised Higher English

by

David Cockburn
Assistant Head Teacher
Inverurie Academy

© D. Cockburn, 1991.
ISBN 0 7169 3160 5

The Scottish Certificate of Education Examination Questions
are reprinted by special permission of
THE SCOTTISH EXAMINATION BOARD

ROBERT GIBSON · Publisher
17 Fitzroy Place, Glasgow, G3 7SF.

INTRODUCTION

This book is intended to be exactly what its title suggests — a practical guide to Revised Higher English. It deals with not only the Folio and the Examination themselves, but also it gives practical advice about the course you will follow and guidance as to how to go about that course.

Like success in everything else in life, success in examinations is in direct proportion to the amount of effort exerted: the more you prepare, the more you are likely to succeed. But you also have to know what to prepare and how to prepare it. This book sets about helping you do both.

I have always felt that the nastiest of the four letter words is "work": there is no substitute for it and certainly no escape from it. Those of your friends who claim to be doing no work are either unsuccessful or inexact. If they are doing well in their subjects, then they are working; if they tell you otherwise, it's their attempt at intellectual machismo. Believe me when I tell you that all success, whether it be academic, sporting, showbiz, model building, designing clothes, or whatever, is dependent on hard work and practice: were there a short cut that avoided work, I would have marketed it and would presently be living idyllically on some paradisical island from the rich proceeds.

You must, then, work hard and put in the hours: if you know what it is you are supposed to be doing and how to do it, you will save energy and time. Being able to budget both is as important, if not more so, than being able to budget money, because both can be just as scarce. This book should help: it will help you plan your course, prepare for your Folio; it will show you how to study literature and write critical essays; it will help you with interpretations and the formal essay; it will see you through the specified texts.

It is meant to be a guide and to be practical. I trust it will be of use.

COPYING PROHIBITED

Note This publication is NOT licensed for copying under the Copyright Licensing Agency's Scheme, to which Robert Gibson & Sons are not party.

All rights reserved. No part of this publication may be reproduced; stored in a retrieval system; or transmitted in any form or by any means — electronic, mechanical, photocopying, or otherwise — without prior permission of the publisher Robert Gibson & Sons, Ltd., 17 Fitzroy Place, Glasgow, G3 7SF.

CONTENTS

CHAPTER I — The Folio of Personal Studies 5
   Review of Personal Reading 5
   Choosing the Text 6
   Your Personal Involvement in the Text 8
   Your Knowledge of the Text 9
   The Time Involved 9
   The Themes *You* See in the Text 10
   The Author's Techniques 11
   Beginning the RPR 12
   Setting Yourself a Task 13
   What are the Examiners looking for? 13
   The Importance of Relevance 15
   A Top Review of Personal Reading 15
   Writing, ... 20
   Imaginative Writing 21
   Discursive Writing 26

CHAPTER II — Close Reading (or Interpretation) 28
   Your own level of maturity 29
   How much you know already about the subject matter 29
   Your own language development 30
   Language and the Way it Works 30
   Grammar 30
   Sentence Structure 34
   Narrative Structure 38
   Punctuation 41
   The Close Reading Passage 44
   Questions about Meaning 45
   Questions which Explore the Ideas of a Passage 45
   Questions about Linkage 45
   Questions about Sentence Structure 46
   Questions about Word-choice 46
   Questions which Ask You to Make Comparisons 47

CHAPTER III — Practical Criticism 49

CHAPTER IV — Specified Texts 55
    Questions which test knowledge of the passage 56
    Questions which deal with the relationship of the
        passage to its immediate context 58
    Questions which deal with the relationship of the
        passage to the work as a whole 58

CHAPTER V — Report or Formal Essay 64
    The Introduction 70
    The Development 71
    The Conclusion 74

CHAPTER VI — Critical Essay 75
    Exclusions 76
    The Approach to the Critical Essay 80
    Conclusion 88

APPENDIX 1 90

APPENDIX 2 93

Chapter I

THE FOLIO OF PERSONAL STUDIES

First of all, you need to know the rules; you need to know exactly what is expected of you when it comes to the Folio. After all, this is the bit of the examination that is totally different from the old Higher, though at least many of you have had some experience of Folio work at Standard Grade.

What, then, have you to do for the Folio? The Scottish Examination Board (SEB) produces a document called *Revised Arrangements in English* which makes clear all the demands or conditions or rules of the examination. If we look at page 12 of Revised Arrangements we shall see what are the demands of the Folio paper:

> Candidates will submit two pieces of writing:
>
> *(a)* a Review of Personal Reading;   (40 marks)
>
> *(b)* **either** a piece of Imaginative Writing
>   or   a piece of Discursive Writing   (25 marks)

Both pieces have to be produced in the course of the year during which you are being presented, and both have to be submitted to the Scottish Examination Board in Dalkeith by 31 March of the year you sit the exam.

Review of Personal Reading

Let's look at the Review of Personal Reading (or RPR) first of all. We shall begin with rules as set out in Revised Arrangements. That document really makes six main points:

(a) it says that your review should "take the form of a detailed study of a single literary text or set of short texts or a comparison of two or more texts";

(b) it goes on to say (and remember this is a rule of the examination) that: "Candidates *will choose their own text(s)* for literary study". I shall return at length to that point.

(c) your choice should be made from imaginative literature, biography, memoirs, essays or journalism;

(d) comparisons may be of a "literary text and its related non-print version" which means that you can compare a novel with the film or television or radio adaptation of that same novel;

(e) you must not use texts which are central to your RPR elsewhere in the examination (see Appendix 2 for the rules of this examination);

(f) your RPR should be between 1000 and 1500 words approximately.

Perhaps the best way forward for us is to take each point in turn and discuss its implications.

I shall assume that you are reading this well before Christmas, and that, therefore, you have time to do the job properly. The key to success in any job is the quantity and quality of the preparation you are willing to undertake. For this job, you are asked to make a *detailed* study of *a single literary text* or *set of short texts* or a *comparison of two or more texts*. You may choose from *imaginative literature* or *biography* or *memoirs* or *essays* or *journalism*. You may, if you wish, make a comparison between a *literary text* and its *related non-print version*.

Choosing the Text

What does all that mean? To begin with you have to choose a text. Now you might need guidance in choosing a text. Your teacher is not allowed to choose it for you, but, after all, your teacher is a well-read individual with a sound knowledge both of books and you, which puts him or her in the ideal position to help. Whatever you do, get away from all the texts you studied last year. Try something new, something different. You should have an idea of the kind of books, plays and poems that you liked last year. Maybe that is where you should begin: by choosing whether to do prose, drama, or poetry. Remember that Revised Arrangements allows you to choose from imaginative literature — and that means not only novels, but plays and poetry as well. In fact, it is true to say that there are too many examples of RPRs based on novels and too few based on plays and poetry. You would undoubtedly do yourself a service if you were to think in terms of genres other than prose — certainly at this stage in your preparation.

Take your time about choosing the text (or texts, if they are short) and seek guidance. You might be tempted to choose a text from popular fiction simply because you find it more accessible than texts which are a bit more demanding. But resist the temptation: you will not be penalised by the Exam Board for choosing *The Guns of Navarone* or *The Great Escape*, but you are likely to penalise yourself by such a choice. You see, the trouble with popular fiction is just that it is not very demanding and that, therefore, it will not offer much in the way of material. Put another way, you will quickly run out of things to say, which isn't very helpful when you have to find around 1500 words.

As well as choosing from poetry, plays and novels, you may also choose from biography, memoirs, essays or journalism: and, most certainly, you must not dismiss any of these options. Look at some of the better travel books (anything by Jonathan Raban or Jan Morris, for example) or at examples of good journalism from the quality press or at a book written about, say, someone you admire, as long as the writing is of quality.

The ideal time to start this procedure of finding a text (or texts) is at the beginning of September because that gives you plenty of time to read, contemplate, and then to choose. When you are in the process of choosing (and remember what I said about including poetry and drama among your options), you should bear in mind a few points since they may well help you make up your mind:

    (a) The book, play or poem (and remember that the book need not be a novel) must interest you — there is no point in writing about a text if it bores you.

Revised Higher English demands evidence of personal interest in and engagement with the text or texts being written about. You have to demonstrate in your RPR (and elsewhere in the Higher) that you *like* the book you are writing about and that it has meant something to you. How can you do that unless you really did like it in the first place?

    (b) The text must be able to provide you with plenty to write about.

As I have already said, a popular text may be easy and enjoyable to read, but it probably won't help you when it comes to writing about it. A text of what is called "literary merit" (and I don't like that term) will at least provide you with sufficient material.

(c) The text must have something to say to you as a person — it must relate in some way to your own individual experiences.

This point is really related to the previous two points, though in many ways I believe it is the most important point. What you must not do is choose any old book that you think will see you through the exercise. This is not an exercise, and any old book will fail you miserably. The RPR is about *personal* reading: "personal" in the sense that you personally chose the text, but "personal" also in the sense that book has special appeal to you *as a person*.

Your Personal Involvement in the Text

Maybe this idea needs a bit more of an explanation. We need to go back to the idea of reading and why we read. There are two main reasons why we read: to *confirm* our experience and to *extend* our experience.

We enjoy a book often because we identify with one of the main characters in it — he/she has the same background as ourselves or is going through the same experiences or is confronted by the same problems. Such books are confirming our experiences, making us a bit more aware of how we feel or how we behave or how we are as people. We are all interested in self and therefore we enjoy these books because they say something about self. In other words, the appeal of such books is very personal — back to that word again.

But there is that other reason for reading: to extend our experience. The novel (or play or poem or travel book or television serial or film) may occupy a world about which we know very little, but about which we are keen to learn; or maybe it involves a character who is experiencing situations or problems or emotions which we have not undergone but by which we are fascinated and in which we are very interested. But we read on because we are interested, because we want to learn or understand: the appeal of a book such as this is still personal.

Now you should choose a book (or play or poem or whatever) for the RPR that has this kind of appeal for you: where it extends or confirms your experience — or, more likely, does both.

Your Knowledge of the Text

Let us now assume that, after some time and a great deal of reading, you have decided on a text which meets the three criteria above: *(a)* it interests you, *(b)* it provides you with plenty to write about, and *(c)* it relates to your own experience. What now? The important thing at this stage is knowledge of the text; you must become very familiar with the book at not only the level of knowledge but also at the level of understanding. I'll explain what I mean by that in a moment, though perhaps you already have an idea of what I mean by the distinction.

The Time Involved

You now have to think in terms of a time-scale. During your Higher course, your teacher may well want you to try a dummy-run at an RPR. If that is the case, then you probably have to produce the dummy-run about Christmas time. If it is now September, that gives you approximately four months in which to do all the preparation, to attempt a couple of drafts for your teacher to go over, and then to produce the final version. If it is now January, you have slightly less time — less than three months — to do the same job for real, though if you have already done a dummy-run then that very practice will save you time since you should have learned from the experience. If you have done a dummy-run, then please do not use the same text for the RPR which is to be sent to the Board; you must try something different since there is little more disagreeable than stirring (or eating) cold porridge. So, whether this is the dummy-run or the real thing, let's say we are thinking in terms of ten weeks. That may seem a lot of time, but remember that you have a writing piece to do as well, and that you have all your other subjects that have just as much claim on your time — and you have a social life to fit in. Most probably, it will take you ten days to a fortnight in which to become familiar with the text itself (or themselves): the level of knowledge. But then you have got to get to the stage of understanding the ideas or issues of the text(s): the level of understanding.

You have spent a week, let's say, becoming familiar with the text and you now feel fairly certain that you have a working knowledge of it. How do you get from this level to the level of understanding? There are three questions to help a reader tackle any work of literature or film or television play or soap opera or whatever:

(ii) What is the novel / travel book / biography / play / poem / film / essay / piece of journalism about?

(ii) What are the effects of the text on me?

(iii) How have these effects been produced?

These questions will provide you with a method of getting from the level of knowledge to the level of understanding the ideas of chosen text and the techniques by which the author expresses these ideas.

The Themes *You* See in the Text

The answer to question (i) will provide you with an idea of the themes or issues of the text. When you answer (i) don't answer in terms of plot: don't simply re-tell the story — you won't be able to re-tell it any better than the author told it in the first place. Answer the question in terms of themes: the novel / book / play / poem / film is about *revenge* or *inadequacy* or *unrequited love* or *greed* or *a teenager's increasing awareness of his/her values* or whatever. Now it is vital to remember that there are no right and/or wrong answers here: what is of utmost importance is that *you* detect these themes in the text. If you detect them, then they are there. Have confidence in yourself, and don't go running to someone else to ask what he or she thinks the book is about.

This point, as I have said, is vital — in every sense of that word! Remember I stressed the importance of your personal reaction to the book — what the book has to say to you as an individual? Well, then, you can see the importance of answering this question in your own terms: the book *to me* is about vaulting ambition — that is what I see in it. And, what is more, I can defend that view when it comes to examining the text.

I feel so strongly about this point. Too many people want to consult others to help form their opinion; some even want to consult the author to ask him what he thinks his book is about! What does it matter what he thinks? Of course, he is entitled to his opinion, but that is all it is — an opinion, one among many. Many authors when interviewed express their surprise that others have detected themes in their work that they themselves have been unaware of. But if the work is good, then it will have all kinds of meaning to all kinds of people, and that is what will make it last. Do you really imagine that an Elizabethan audience, sitting (or more likely standing) in the bitter chill of some November day over four hundred years ago, got exactly the same meaning out of *Hamlet* as a modern Elizabethan audience does today? Our society is different, our culture is different, our attitudes to authority are different, our values about love, sexuality and responsibility are different. Our perception of Hamlet, himself, must be different from the first Elizabethan one, if for no other reason than that Freud has come in between.

We really can have little idea how an Elizabethan audience viewed *Hamlet*, but we can be sure that it would be different from one today. And that is a huge tribute to the play — that it is so rich in meaning that it can relate to audiences as diverse as 400 years apart or 4000 miles apart.

What matters, then, is you and your relationship with the text and not someone else's relationship with it, even if that someone else is the author.

What about the answer to question (ii) — What are the effects of the text on me? The answer to this question is in terms of your reaction to the text. The printed word (or the celluloid image) has the capacity to make us laugh, cry, feel happy, feel sad, feel pity, feel anger, and even, at times, feel bored. Again we are talking about *your* reaction: *your* laughter, *your* tears, *your* happiness. And these emotions are just as real as the emotions you have in "real" life. What you feel when you read (or watch a film) is related then to your experience of real life, and that experience is both private and unique to you.

We all have to learn to trust our emotional reactions to texts: what is happening is that the text is re-patterning, re-organising our experience. We take our experience to the text and the text is re-shaping that experience for us. How does the text re-shape our experience?

The Author's Techniques

That question leads us into the interesting area of technique: the ways in which an author creates effect. No doubt you will have noticed that that is the subject of question (iii) — How have the effects been produced?

Any work of art — and in this context it doesn't matter a jot that the work of art is literature — any work of art is artificial: someone somewhere has put it together using either words or paint or musical notation or marble or plastic. The creator or artist has taken decisions about how the thing can best be put together in order to create an effect or effects. What we as critics have to do is, with great skill, to examine *how* it has been put together. What we are talking about, of course, is the skill of Practical Criticism, and from Practical Criticism there is no escape when it comes to the intelligent reading of literature. You see, the intelligent and *meaningful* reading of a book is not to find out what someone else has said about it; it is to read it aware of your own reactions to it, and to discover by means of this sensitive reading how — the ways in which — the author has created these reactions in you. This is not to destroy literature (or painting or music or sculpture) by cold analysis, but actually to enrich it by enabling you to discover the many layers of meaning embedded in the text.

Beginning the RPR

This all seems to have taken us a long way from September. Or was it January? But in effect it hasn't. You really do need to digest and understand what I have said previously in order to be able to begin the process of coming to terms with the text you have chosen for you RPR. By now you have read it and have begun to ask yourself questions (ii) and (iii).

Next, you need a jotter or notebook. Write down your initial answers to (i) in the notebook. We have now established the themes, ideas, issues the text has for you. What were some of your initial reactions — answers to question (ii) — again jot them down before you forget. Now go back to the text with your answer to (i) — the issues, ideas, themes. Take one of these themes you have written down. How does this theme get established? Go back to the text and examine it closely to ascertain where the theme and how the theme is established. Is it right at the beginning? Is it with the introduction of a character? Does the author use any symbolism — images that you might associate with the theme? You will get the hang of this if you look at *The Practical Guide to Higher Literature* where there is an examination of how themes are established in the opening chapter of Graham Greene's *The Power and the Glory*. You will see there that it isn't particularly difficult to do this kind of thing and it really does enrich your reading of the text. Such careful reading reveals a great deal more of what is there than you first suspect.

You have now begun the work for your RPR in earnest.

You need to go ahead and repeat what we have just done, this time for all the themes that you have noted in your book. Keep everything together in your book for handy reference later. That will take up a lot of time, but remember what I said about preparation: the more work you do now, the easier will be the writing stage. Now think in terms of your answers to (ii) — the effects on you: you need to note your emotional reactions to the text. The next stage is the important one: the answers to (iii). You know what your reactions to the text are, but you now need to work out how — the techniques by which — the author has created these reactions in you. Once you have done all that — and for further advice about how to set about the task, please see *The Practical Guide to Literature* — you are then ready to begin the business of writing your first draft of your RPR.

Setting Yourself a Task

However, before you put pen to paper, you have to decide on the *task*. You see, the mistake that far too many candidates make is to assume all that is wanted is a kind of vague, directionless book review. I cannot tell you plainly enough that that is not what is wanted, and in fact such reviews, no matter how well written, must fail. The Revised Arrangements document states very clearly that there has to be a line of argument running through the RPR, and a woolly book review cannot have a line of argument running through it. The way to ensure that you have a line of argument is to set yourself a task — set out to prove a case, and make sure your RPR does just that.

What kind of task, then, is suitable for an RPR? The answer really depends on the kind of notes you have already made. By now you know what your reactions to the text are, you know the themes you have detected in it, and you know how the author has established both. You should have an idea what you want to say, and you need the kind of task that will allow you to say it.

What are the Examiners looking for?

I shall go over later in detail what it is the examiners are looking for, but there are some points that are worth mentioning now because they may have a bearing on the kind of task you eventually choose to do. Firstly, the examiners are looking for *knowledge of the text*: you have to demonstrate that you have read the text and that you are familiar with it. That, of course, does not mean that you simply re-tell the story as evidence that you have read the book. You demonstrate your knowledge of the text *implicitly* as you fulfil the task you set yourself.

Secondly, as well as knowledge of the text, examiners are looking for an understanding of the ideas of the text: you have to be able to show that you understand the issues raised by the text and have a grasp of the themes as you see them. If you have planned the work as I have suggested then that will be easy for you.

Thirdly, examiners are looking for an understanding of the techniques deployed by the author: again, if you have done your work as above then this should be no trouble to you. You should be aware of the techniques before you start writing.

Fourthly, examiners are looking for a genuine personal interest in the chosen material. That is why I have stressed all along that what matters is what you see in the material, and as long as you can justify what it is you see by reference to the text, then you will do well.

Your task, then, must allow you to demonstrate all four points:

(a) knowledge of the text;

(b) understanding of the ideas in the text;

(c) understanding of techniques used in the text;

(d) genuine personal interest.

Once you have decided on your task, check with your teacher that it is appropriate. He/she is not allowed to set the task for you, but, as an expert, he/she is best able to advise you as to whether or not the task will serve its purpose. If, however, you are really stuck and cannot think of anything to set yourself, you could, as a last resort, have a look at past papers, either for Unrevised Paper III or Revised Paper II, to see the kind of tasks examiners have set in the past. At least these papers may give you the basis for an idea — but once you have decided check with your teacher before you start writing.

The Importance of Relevance

Once you have decided on your task, you can begin writing. Make sure that the task is clearly and unambiguously expressed in the opening paragraph of your RPR, such that anyone reading the first paragraph (particularly the marker) will be totally aware of what it is you are about to do.

Thereafter make sure that you refer back to your task frequently — that will help to keep you relevant — and make sure that, whenever you make a point about the text, you support that point by close reference to what the author has actually said. You are in effect performing the same writing task as you will perform in Paper II — Critical Essay: you are writing about literature. The only difference is that the RPR is an extended piece of writing and you have the text in front of you for consultation and accurate reference. All this means, of course, that the skills you are developing in writing the RPR will be the skills you will need when it comes to sitting Paper II, Part 2 in the exam itself. Nothing need be wasted.

A Top Review of Personal Reading

Many people, including teachers, ask what a really good RPR looks like. Well I can tell you. The following RPR was awarded top marks — $^{40}/_{40}$ — by the examiners, and I think you will see why. Note that it does everything I have suggested you should do, so if you do it, you can't go wrong!

'The Crucible' as a Tragedy

> Before I had ever seen or read Arthur Miller's play *The Crucible*, I had heard what it was supposed to be about. Yet when I saw a production of *The Crucible* at the Citizens Theatre in Glasgow in September 1989, I found my attention gripped, my mind stirred and my emotions aroused not by a play about events in the America of the 1950s, nor by an allegory of them, nor by a play making an overt political point; what I saw unfolding was the story of a man — a man, John Proctor, who is respected within his community, but who has sinned greatly and with awful results: a man whose failings, combined with terrifying developments in his community, lead him to his death — and in so doing to find a new belief in himself and bring truth and hope to his society and ours. I came away from the theatre feeling a mixture of emotions; anger, horror and disbelief about the witch-hunts, pity for and empathy with John and Elizabeth Proctor and with other characters, and hope and gladness, a strong feeling

that the end was right. In other words I had experienced a tragedy. Many people see *The Crucible* mainly in terms of the witch-hunts and their political significance, but for me they were essentially the background to the story of the two main characters, providing the crucible, the ordeal which they go through. I was moved by the human beings and their fates, and so in this piece of writing I will talk about the tragedy of John and Elizabeth Proctor.

John Proctor, the tragic hero of *The Crucible*, is a man of apparent strength, both physically and in his opinions and manner, a man who makes up his own mind and keeps it, and has strong common sense and a sense of right. This we can see in Act I, in which we see Proctor as the people of Salem see him in ordinary times: here these aspects of his character are apparent along with his contempt for the foolish and paranoid Parris and power-greedy Thomas Putnam in his argument with the two men, and the awe, almost fear, which he inspires in his servant Mary Warren shows us the effect which he can have on people.

However, in Act I we are also made aware of Proctor's failing, the sin which he has committed before the time at which the play opens; he has felt lust for, and then slept with, a girl, Abigail Williams, who worked as a servant in his house. This failing fills Proctor with great depths of shame, anger and guilt and he sees himself as a hypocrite. All these feelings are concentrated in two main emotions which are developed and resolved in the play. Firstly, Proctor feels himself to be a fraud because of the discrepancy between his outwardly respectable image and his inner view of himself. In a man who is, as Act I shows us, usually bluntly open about his feelings, this weighs particularly heavy. Secondly, he feels guilt. Guilt is not just an acknowledgement that the code of a society has been broken; if we feel guilty, if we feel guilt within ourselves, we know that what we have done is wrong by our own standards. Salem was a deeply puritanical community where life was hard and basic (the harshness of the life was shown very effectively in the production I saw by the very bare wooden set and the actors' all-black clothing). Ploughing on Sunday was considered by some a serious matter so the crime of "lechery" would provoke horror and disgust perhaps difficult for a modern reader to understand. Proctor, although not accepting the moral and religious code blindly — he would plough on Sunday and feel no guilt, for it does not contravene his own moral code — is a deeply religious man with a strong sense of right. He judges his own failing as severely as his community would, for he has sinned against his own morality, indeed more severely because he is a better man than many in Salem and it is to have such terrible effects. Because he realises his own failing and condemns himself for it, guilt manifests itself in Proctor as a lack of self-worth amounting to self-disgust.

When we have feelings like Proctor's, we do not want to keep feeling them; it is our instinct and our desire to lose them, by removing the circumstance which causes them or, if that is not possible, by atoning for them in some way.

This resolution of each of Proctor's two main feelings gives us the main climaxes of the play. But before each of these comes a scene between John and his wife Elizabeth in which the state of mind of each is shown most clearly. Then at the end of the scene the intervention of other characters into the action forces Proctor to acknowledge his feelings and gives him a way to resolve them.

The relationship between John and Elizabeth is vital to the tragedy of *The Crucible*; the scenes between them function as I have said above, the bad aspects, the failings in the marriage contribute to John's failing and the good points in it help each to find resolution of and atonement for their failings. Elizabeth is a "good woman": her failing is that she is too ready to acknowledge her own goodness — "I am a good woman", she says — and to judge harshly its presence or absence in others. She also finds it difficult to express emotion, especially love, and this apparent coldness helped turn John to Abigail. These failings and the failings in the marriage to which they contribute are shown in the first scene between the Proctors. In Act II, and here we also see that John, trying to atone for the hurt he gave to Elizabeth by his sin in the only way open to him at that time, by trying to please her, and pushed into a resentful defensiveness by her attitude, is not reaching and acknowledging the depth of his own feelings of guilt and hypocrisy and has no real way to resolve them. "I mean to please you, Elizabeth", John says, and goes to kiss her. The stage directions say "She receives it. With a certain disappointment he returns to the table." As "a sense of their separation rises" (stage directions), their conversation turns to Abigail and the witch-hunts. "I do not judge you, John" Elizabeth says: but in her heart she does and Proctor senses it. His response is angry, and made more so by what he must know at his depths, that this "atonement" is not really such, is not sufficient: "I have gone tiptoe in this house all seven month since [Abigail] is gone. I have not moved from there to here without I think to please you, and still an everlasting funeral marches round your heart."

The arrival of court officials with a warrant for Elizabeth's arrest heralds a turning point in the play. It is an extra twist to the tragedy in *The Crucible* that the background events which lead Proctor to his death are to some extent caused by him; Abigail accuses Elizabeth of witchcraft because she hopes and believes, since Proctor has proved that he "thought softly of her", that he will marry her if his wife is dead. This confrontation with the horrific effects of his sin and the obvious fact that he has not atoned for it at all brings Proctor's two main feelings to the surface. His anguish of self-disgust is expressed in desperate attempts at avoiding further pain for his wife: "Damn you, man, you will not chain her... I will not have her chained!" But his love for his wife is also brought to the surface and gives him the determination to take action which provides him with a chance to resolve his first feeling, that of being a fraud; in order to save Elizabeth, he must expose Abigail, and if he exposes Abigail's sin he must expose his own. Although he will have to face public horror and shame, the pretence will at last be over. The Act finishes with his resolve to do this despite the retribution which will fall on him: "Now Hell and Heaven grapple on our backs, and all our old pretence is ripped away . . . It is a providence and no great change; we are as we always were, but naked now . . . And God's icy wind will blow!"

Those words provide a dramatic climax. But the minor climax of the tragedy occurs in Act III, when Proctor actually achieves resolution of his fraud; for his love of Elizabeth, he admits his lechery to the court. In the same scene Elizabeth also achieves a resolution and recognition of her failings; the woman who would never lie, who has prized her own goodness above all else to the detriment of her marriage, sacrifices her pure morality for love of her husband — to protect John, she lies and says he never slept with Abigail. Both have gone through the first part of the crucible.

However both still have overwhelming feelings and failings to resolve. The scene between them in Act IV, three months on, provides a contrast to that of Act II; Proctor admits his depth of guilt and self-disgust and his feeling that he cannot atone for his sin, and Elizabeth admits her own failings and their part in John's sin — and with this their relationship is reforged. "I have my own sins to count. It needs a cold wife to prompt lechery" she admits. "I never knew how I should say my love. It were a cold house I kept!" When she now says "I cannot judge you, John", she means it, feels it truly from her heart: she has realised that she herself has failings and thus learned not to judge others. The new warmth, the new start which her resolution brings, is symbolised by her pregnancy. For Elizabeth the only right atonement is to live in a better way than she has done before: but John now moves with anguish to his own resolution, the final dramatic and tragic climax of the play. Proctor is filled with guilt for his sin and this makes him feel great self-disgust. His inner self desperately seeks a resolution of that self-disgust, an atonement for the cause of the guilt; he needs to do something which is prompted by the goodness and strength in his character and will allow him to see that these qualities can balance out his failing and wash out the guilt, something which is the cause of good and truth and thus atones for his sin and fraud. His death for refusing to sign a false confession to witchcraft, which might help to lead the community to see the madness which it is caught up in and which chooses the path of God and truth, would achieve this for him. However, Proctor decides to confess because he simply does not believe that he has it in him to die like this and is determined not to recommence the fraud. He compares himself unfavourably with the other martyrs, Rebecca Nurse, Martha Corey, the comical old man Giles Corey who gained new dignity in his death: "Let them that never lied die now to keep their souls. It is pretence for me". He does not recognise that good and strength may exist alongside sin and weakness in a man's character — he does not recognise his own strength and goodness, shown in his public confession to lechery, and which has always been present in him: "I cannot mount the gibbet like a saint. It is a fraud. I am not that man." "I am no good man. Nothing's spoiled by giving them this lie that were not rotten long before." But the truth will out, the truth of Proctor's soul cannot be denied. His literal inability to sign the confession and see it stand as his record — "I have given you my soul: leave my name!" he cries and tears up his confession — allows him to see his own worth at last, and perhaps in so doing to realise that there was never any real fraud: "I do think I see some shred of goodness in John Proctor" he says in wonder. As he is led to the scaffold for his atonement, Reverend Hale cries "What profit him to bleed? Shall the worms declare his truth?" But it is only by dying that Proctor can realise his goodness and keep his soul. Life is not worth having and preserving at all costs; Proctor's life would be worth little to him if he felt that he was "rotten" and that he was only alive because he was not good enough to die.

And so Proctor's death, and the end of the play, leaves us with that mixture of emotions which a tragedy provokes: I was horrified by the circumstances of the death yet I willed Proctor not to sign the confession which would save his life, because I wanted him to see his own worth. Elizabeth's words express the conflicting feelings which all audiences must share: "I want you living, John. That's sure" she says, but her final cry, the last line of the play, recognises the rightness of his death: "He have his goodness now. God forbid I take it from him!" The hero's resolution and atonement, which allow him to find his true self, and the conflicting emotions which they provoke are the essence of the tragedy.

The main dramatic and emotional effect of *The Crucible* can only be felt by watching a performance of it. But reading the play enabled me to add depth of comprehension to the emotional impact of seeing it on the stage. In trying to understand the story of one man which had struck me so forcibly in September, I came to understand a whole play — and in understanding that, I have begun to learn and understand much more still.

There are a few tiny flaws, but they do nothing to detract from the excellence of this piece. It shows thorough knowledge of the text, it shows not only a thorough understanding of the play, but, indeed, shows how the writer's understanding was enhanced by the experience of the performance, and it shows an awareness of the writer's techniques. The task is clearly stated and adhered to throughout. An examiner couldn't really wish for anything more, and, indeed, it is exactly what the examiners are looking for.

Of course you don't need to go to a performance of a play in order to produce an excellent RPR: just bear in mind some of the lessons you have so far learned. And remember that the highest marks will go to those RPR's which demonstrate beyond doubt the genuineness of the candidate's involvement in the text. But maybe it is also worth pointing out that you don't have to be this good to pass the RPR!

There is one thing you must bear in mind, however: the text that is central to your RPR may not be used elsewhere in the examination.

But perhaps it is time to turn our minds to the writing task, which is also part of the Folio of Personal Studies.

Writing

One of the main advantages of this exam is that your essay can be done in your own time (although the final copy must be done in school under supervision).

As with the RPR, the first thing we'll do is look at the Revised Arrangements document to see what the rules are about Writing. It says that you may choose to do either Imaginative Writing or Discursive Writing. The document states:

> *Imaginative Writing*
>
> Candidates will choose their own topic for the piece of imaginative writing in consultation with the supervising teacher, who will advise on suitability. The piece must take *one* of the following forms:
>
> an essay reflecting on personal experience;
>
> a piece of prose fiction (e.g. short story/episode from novel);
>
> a poem;
>
> a dramatic script (e.g. scene, monologue, sketch).
>
> The length of the piece should be appropriate to the form chosen. The final draft must be done in the presenting centre under the teacher's supervision. This does not mean that it needs to be completed under formal examination conditions. Only the final version should be submitted.

The document goes on to say:

Discursive Writing

Candidates will choose their own topic for the piece of Discursive Writing in consultation with the supervising teacher, who will advise on its suitability. Candidates will be required to produce an extended piece of continuous prose of approximately 600 – 800 words. While reading, note-taking and early drafting may be undertaken outwith the presenting centre, the final draft must be done in the centre under the teacher's supervision: this does not mean that it needs to be completed under formal examination conditions. Only the final version should be submitted.

We really do need to take each of these a stage at a time. Again, your final mark will very much depend on the amount you put in to the preparation of your writing piece.

Imaginative Writing

When most people think of imaginative writing, they think of the short story, but we must remember here that much more is meant than just the short story. The SEB itself identifies four areas in its Arrangements document (see above). Let's take each in turn.

An essay Reflecting on Personal Experience

Some of the best work done, particularly by those candidates who do not claim to be brilliant at English, is done as the personal essay. Personal essays are those where the candidate writes about his or her own experiences in a reflective way.

There is, after all, no subject that we know more about than "ourselves" and therefore the problem of knowledge does not occur in the way in which it does with the discursive essay: there is no argument to present. Nor are we faced with the problem of form as we are when it comes to writing a short story or a poem. There is really no special skill to be learned and practised. But remember, you may be fascinated by yourself and think yourself the most riveting person on the planet, but others may not agree. You know yourself from experience that there is nothing more boring than the anecdotal ramblings of a tedious egocentric. A personal essay *must* have shape; it must be planned; it must be reflective.

A Piece of Prose Fiction (e.g. Short Story/Episode from a Novel)

In many ways the candidate we have been speaking about, the one who would like to get a "B" pass and maybe even an "A" pass, should think very seriously about this area for his or her writing piece. Either this area or the discursive essay — these are the two serious contenders for such a candidate's attention. Meantime let's concentrate on the short story. Naturally, anyone embarking on a short story must have knowledge of the short story form, but then you can hardly have got through five years of a secondary school English course and not know about the form of the short story. What really matters in the short story is economy of style: the writer makes every word, every scene, every bit of symbolism count. There is no room here for padding. Moreover, the ending takes on special significance in the short story: not that it has to have some peculiar twist — only some short stories are like that — but it does have to be "telling". All this means that any short story has to be well-plotted and well-planned. The marvellous thing about this examination is that you have every chance to plot and plan your work — you have nearly six months (or more) to work on it. And there is much evidence in what the candidates actually produce that the short story form is being taken seriously, with endings that have been cleverly thought out well before the stage of final drafts.

Here is an example of a short story which is by no means perfect, but it has satisfied some of the conditions I have suggested above: it shows evidence of planning, and certainly of the ending having been thought out beforehand. It is a conscious piece of writing, by which I mean that the writer is aware of the effects that can be gained by careful structuring and by careful word-choice. It is certainly an attempt to exploit the short story form; it definitely creates tension, as I think you will agree.

GUSSIE'S PARCEL

It was a brown parcel, tied up with string: the same stuff that mum used for her plants. It was quite soft and squidgy, and yet heavy when picked up. What looked like a red hand was printed on the top of the parcel. Gussie's small fingers clenched around the knot. He sat cross-legged on the floor, fighting with this disobedient lump. Finally a piece of string gave, the rest flowed off onto the floor leaving the parcel free. Gussie looked around guiltily. He listened. The day was just beginning; cars had begun to roam the streets, producing swish-burr noises as they passed the house. Louder then softer ... louder then softer ... He whipped off the brown paper. Mummy wasn't up yet. Inside was a bundly of newspaper, loose around some heavy object inside. A gleam of something black, shiny and cold caught Gussie's attention. The newspaper fell off leaving a large metal object in his small hands. Gussie recognised it at once. His heartbeat quickened.

Gussie was only a small boy; at the stage when lorries, tractors, the sandpit in the back yard and 'Cowboys 'n' Injuns' still dominated his life. Especially Cowboys and indians. There was nothing Gussie liked more than to play a good long game of Cowboys and Indians with dad, or mum. Dad was 'away' at the moment, so Gussie had to make do with playing with mum. Mum was good at playing, but she often had other 'things' to do.

He was one of those boys who always get up early in the mornings, relishing the hour of play before breakfast, it seemed, more than any other of the day. Perhaps it had something to do with the fact that it was the only time of the day when he was left truely unsupervised. Only he must keep quiet; that was the golden rule.

Of course Gussie was often up when the mail arrived through the letterbox. He would always give it a look over, just as a matter of course. On the most part it was boring letters:— the floppy ones with windows, through which you could see dull square writing. Sometimes there'd be a picture card. That was fun, but even it lost its appeal after a while.

So Gussie had been rather surprised and excited that day when he saw the parcel, lying there on the hallway floor. He knew he shouldn't touch the mail, or open any of it, but a parcel like this was chance not to be missed. Besides it had no writing on it, just that peculiar red hand (at least it looked like a hand), so anyone was allowed to open it. It was probably for him anyway. All the same he did feel a bit guilty as he unwrapped the parcel.

But now, as he held this magnificent-looking thing in his hands, all thoughts and fears about what mum would do if she caught him vanished. Instead he was left with a fluttering excitement. A gun! It must have been for him after all. Perhaps daddy had sent him another present:— a gun just like the one he used! It was so much better than the one he'd got for Christmas. That was nothing compared to this. That had a shiny, silvery barrel and plastic handle. It was rather light as well, even for Gussie. The shine had been knocked off in places anyway and it didn't click as well as it used to. But this!... This was great! It was cold, sleek and black. There was'nt a scratch on it. It was beautifully heavy, exactly like dad's!

Gussie began to examine the gun carefully. How strange! It had two triggers! The usual one, and another smaller one, stuck to the side of the gun. It wasn't a proper one — it was too small and straight — but it was interesting all the same. Gussie saw that he could flick this trigger from one side to another, clicking it as he did so. He left it in its original position. Mum was always going on about leaving things as you found them.

Gussie was interrupted by noises from upstairs. Mum was getting up. Time had lapsed since he first saw the parcel. The light had already begun to change from blues and greys to yellows and reds. A beautiful idea sprang into Gussie's head.

He ran back upstairs as quickly, and quietly, as he could. The next thing mum would do would be to go to the bathroom. He could hear her humming in the bedroom; she only did that when she was properly awake and getting dressed. Gussie crept into the bathroom and hid behind the door. He waited.

Presently he heard mum's bedroom door open. Footsteps crossed the landing. The light flicked on and mum came into the room. She went over to the basin, her back towards him. Now he'd do it! Wouldn't she get a fright! Gussie chuckled inwardly to himself. Mum had started to run the tap and was reaching out for the toothpaste. Gussie hopped out of his hiding place.

"Yaa! Got ye injun!" Gussie recited the usual western talk from the films. "Git yer hands up!" His mother swung round.

"Oh Gussie dear, it's you! What a fright you gave me! You must stop creeping up on me like that." But then a change came over her. Her face grew rigid and pale. "What is that you've got in your hand? Where did you get it from?"

"It's mine. A present from dad. Isn't it great!" Gussie waved his gun in emphasis. "I found a parcel downstairs." But mum was acting strangely. Her usual cheery look had disappeared from her face; she didn't even have her scolding look, or anything that Gussie had ever seen before. Gussie felt distinctly uneasy.

"Put it down at once!" Her voice quavered with great effort.

"Why? It is mine, isn't it?" Gussie tried to continue with his game, eager to return to known territory: "Come on injun, git yer hands up!" His voice was full of uncertainty. There was a pause.

"All...all right...I...I'll play ... But don't fire the gun: it'll wake the neighbours." She raised her hands, jerkily. For some reason Gussie still felt uneasy. But at least she was playing the game properly now. He had the strange feeling of having mum under his power, as though he was stronger than her. It was almost as if she were afraid of him. Gussie didn't like this feeling at all; it was alien to him. Above all it was the unknown. His face creased up in painful thought.

"Gussie dear . . . Can we stop now? It...it's breakfast time ... Give me your gun, there's a good boy. It' so......beautiful (the word came out hideous and twisted) . . . Can I have a look at it?

Gussie's round little face scrumpled up, his brows stood out in concentration. Indecision took hold.

There are a number of faults in this piece of writing, one of which is that there really is insufficient reference to Ireland for the reader to get the point immediately. It is, however, well above average, and it was awarded $^{21}/_{25}$ by the examiners — a very respectable mark. You see what can be done with a little effort?

A Poem

If the short story should be thought of as a serious possibility, a poem should be thought of in the same terms as the plague. Fortunately, very few candidates attempt poetry for their writing piece, and those who have done have no doubt regretted it the July following its submission. In order to attempt poetry you really have to be very good at it, and, what is more, you really have to be recognised as being good at it. You need to know about verse structure, rhythm, rhyme, sound, and all kinds of poetic techniques. If you seriously do want to produce poetry for your writing piece, you would do well to have a look at *The Practical Guide to Poetry* published by Robert Gibson & Sons: it will make clear to you that there is much more to poetry than most people assume!

A Dramatic Script

So far in the history of Revised Higher, there have been very few examples of dramatic scripts produced. What is true of poetry would also be true of dramatic script: you need to know what you are doing, and you need to have done it successfully in the past.

Discursive Writing

One significant aspect of Higher English is the sheer amount of discursive writing demanded. You need to be able to write discursively throughout Paper II — in the Report and in the Critical Essay. Since, then, discursive writing is a skill that you must master to do well anyway, it would seem sensible to think of it as a serious option for this part of the examination. Here is the opportunity to set out on paper an issue about which you feel strongly. Here is the opportunity to research the issue so that you can support your ideas with facts and references. Here you can meaningfully explore your own views while taking account of the views of others.

Discursive writing, however, is not just about issues and views and arguments: it is also about how to set out an argument, about marshalling ideas and thoughts, and about precision in the use of language in expressing these arguments. Too many candidates do badly in the discursive essay because they have not learned how to set one out. Not that there is a special formula — nothing would contribute more to the death of good prose — but there is a technique.

First of all, you have to decide on a topic and then research it thoroughly, which means trips to the library or to wherever you can find the information. It may mean writing to companies, institutions or individuals. Once you have located the information, you have to take notes from it. (Again, your little notebook will prove invaluable: in fact, you should keep the back of the notebook as a place to record vocabulary items the meaning of which you don't know in order to increase your store of words.) Then you must begin the process of evaluating the information you have to hand. You must decide on a line of argument, and then, using the evaluated material, you must plan how to present that argument to its best effect. That means introducing the argument, and that might be most effectively done by an anecdote or by a short concrete example, so that you are moving from the particular to the general. If you look carefully at the essays of George Orwell, you will see that often he begins discursive material in this way.

Once the material has been introduced, bearing in mind that your reader may not be the expert you are and may not therefore have the understanding that you have, you then must set out your argument, supporting it, as always, by facts, statistics, or evidence. You must take account of the opposing argument, demonstrating that you have thought of its implications but that you can counter it effectively. The next stage is then to conclude the argument. You don't want to be introducing new material into your conclusion, but neither do you want merely to repeat what you have just said in a shortened form: here is the opportunity to round off you argument using language effectively and precisely such that you leave your reader impressed by your skills. Maybe it is the place to return to your anecdote at the beginning, or to refer to some other concrete material or, indeed, to end on a note so general that it amounts, almost, to a universal proposition. Whatever else, make sure that you pay attention to the rhythm of your final sentence: it has to end with resounding effect.

The mistake most candidates make when it comes to discursive essays is to ignore argument and evidence in favour of venting forth their feelings in a most splenetive and rash manner, with invective, thoughtlessness, and blind prejudice being peddled as rational thought.

To gain a top mark for a discursive essay, you must display fairly sophisticated skills: your chosen subject must be treated in depth; you must show a sound knowledge of and real interest in what you are arguing; and that argument has to be developed and sustained. You have to demonstrate a skilful control of paragraphing, sentence structure and punctuation, and a precision in language that shows an awareness of the structuring of ideas. Your vocabulary should be extensive and appropriate and your prose crisp and clear.

These may seem skills too complex to be bothered about: but remember what I said about the amount of discursive prose demanded by this examination. These skills, no matter how daunting the mastery of them may seem to you at the moment, are nevertheless well worth acquiring.

Folio of Personal Studies

We have now gone over all the main points about the Folio, both from your point of view and the point of view of the examiner. Spend a great deal of time on this Chapter, and spend a great deal of preparation time on your folio: it is worth 65 marks — one third of the total for the examination — and since it is work that is prepared, drafted and redrafted over several months, it should be of your very best, and it should make a huge contribution to your final award.

Chapter II

CLOSE READING (or INTERPRETATION)

The examination itself consists of two papers each of one hour fifty minutes duration and each worth 65 marks.

The first paper (Paper I) is called "Reading" and is in two parts:

Part 1

> This will be a test of close reading. In any one year there will be an unseen prose passage of substantial length or two equivalent unseen prose passages on a topic of general interest drawn from fiction or non-fiction. The non-fiction sources will include quality journalism, the literature of travel or history or science or the arts, essays and biography /memoir.

Part 2

> This will also be a test of reading. It will contain two sections. Candidates will choose one section only, A or B. Section A will contain a previously unseen poem, piece of prose or dramatic dialogue with associated questions. Section B will contain a key passage from each of the specified prose or dramatic texts. It will also contain a complete poem, or a key passage from a poem, from each of the specified sets of poems. Each passage and poem will be accompanied by its own set of associated questions. Candidates choosing Section B will attempt the question on *one* of these key passages or poems. The question will test candidates' knowledge of the passage, its immediate context and its relationship to the text as a whole. For poetry, questions will also test awareness of relationships with other poem(s) in the specified set.

In this Chapter, we shall look at close reading or interpretation.

The interpretation (or close reading) paper in Revised Higher sets out to test your ability to understand a piece of English and to test your knowledge of how language is used. Such knowledge and understanding, it has to be stressed, are not acquired overnight. Close reading is designed to test sophisticated, high-level reading skills, which can only be developed as a product of a five- or six-year English course at Secondary School. Moreover, reading skills depend on other factors such as your interests, how much you know already about the subject being written about, and on the level of your own language development.

Let's take each of these factors in turn:

Your own level of maturity

"Maturity" is a difficult concept to define, but it has to do with the kinds of things you, as a human being, have experienced and on your capacities to learn from those experiences. As we mature and become more aware of the experience of reading, our reading skills improve. We shall come back to this point later.

How much you know already about the subject matter.

Undoubtedly, a piece of writing makes more sense to us if we already know something about its subject matter. For example, an English teacher might well have great difficulty in understanding his Chemistry colleague's PhD thesis, whereas that same English teacher whose one passion in life is politics would have little difficulty with a Sunday newspaper article speculating about the skills or otherwise of some controversial all-party committee report on toxic taxes. Similarly, you would find an article about some aspect of your favourite hobby presents you with little difficulty, whereas an article about the lack of pronouns in modern Turkish might turn out to be a bit beyond you — unless, of course, you're a linguist and your name is Hasan.

But, again, the point won't have escaped you — and it is linked to what has already been said about experience and maturity: the more subjects in which you become interested, the wider your reading will become, and therefore the more sense you will make of it. The day will soon come when you look forward avidly to the thud of that quality newspaper on your doormat every Sunday; maybe that day has already arrived.

Your own language development

The importance of the continuing development of our language skills cannot be overstressed. You have to go on adding words to your vocabulary, learning to distinguish subtle differences in meaning, developing ways of expressing your thoughts and feelings, generally becoming more aware of acquiring new language skills. And this is a two-way process: reading will help develop all your language skills, and as you develop them, the more sophisticated your reading skills will become. A kind of upward spiral. One of the best ways of acquiring and developing these skills is for you to read a quality newspaper at least once a week.

LANGUAGE AND THE WAY IT WORKS

Grammar

But let's take a closer look at language and how it works. English is a word-ordered language: meaning is dependent on the order of words in a given sentence. For example

        The boy loves the girl

doesn't mean the same as

        The girl loves the boy

precisely because of the order of the words. Not all languages work in the same way. In some languages the meaning is determined by the ending of the word. For example, if we translate the firsts sentence into Latin

        Puer amat puellam

and then play around with the order

        Puellam amat puer

the sentence will still mean the same because the "-am" ending in "puellam" tells the reader that it is the girl who is loved. English used to be like that — meaning in English used to be dependent on word endings. We call such languages *inflected languages*. There are still some words in modern English which retain the ending related to meaning: for example, *who*, *whose*, *whom*. But what matters in modern English is the order in which the words occur. Take the sentence,

>I drove up the street and stopped at the lights.

The words in this sentence form a pattern which you recognise; the pattern of them we call "grammar". I can alter that pattern a little:

>Up the High Street I drove and at the lights I stopped

and you will still recognise the re-arrangement as meaningful. I can still alter it a bit more:

>The High Street I drove up and at the lights stopped I

without stretching your incredulity too much. But you would have difficulty with:

>I Street up High drove lights stopped I and the the at.

The reason you have difficulty with the last arrangement is that I have broken completely the rules of the pattern, the rules of grammar.

It is these rules which govern the way in which we arrange words to make the pattern meaningful.

You need also to know a few labels for words since these labels make talking about sentence structure much easier.

(a) A *verb* is a word which relates to actions. For example,

>I *visited* the boutique and *bought* a tie.

Both "visited" and "bought" are words associated with action, and we label such words *verbs*. You need to know about verbs because they will be referred to later in this book. The association with action is, however, fairly loose, so keep your wits about you when you are trying to identify a verb in a sentence.

I <u>think</u> that she <u>is</u> very clever <u>to be able</u> to <u>dance</u> like that.

Although "to dance" is clearly associated with action, "think" and "is" and "to be able" are less obviously so, yet all three are verbs.

(b) A *noun* is the name of a thing or a person. For example,

The <u>boy</u> talked to the <u>girl</u> outside the <u>disco</u>.

The underlined words — "boy", "girl" and "disco" are names, and we label such names *nouns*.

(c) A *pronoun* is a word which stands for a noun: *I, he, she, it, we, you, they*. Pronouns will present you with few difficulties.

(d) An *adjective* is a word which describes things or people. For example,

There were (ten) (green) bottles on the (wet) bar.

The words which have been circled are *adjectives*, that is, they are words which describe the noun which follows: the "bottles" are described by the number adjective "ten" and the colour adjective "green"; the "bar" is described as being "wet".

Notice that in English (as in other languages) there is an order for the number and colour adjectives: the number adjective comes before any other adjective and is therefore furthest away from the noun it describes, whereas the colour adjective always comes right beside the noun it describes: you cannot meaningfully say —

There were green beautiful fifteen bottles on the shelf.

(e) An *adverb* is a word which changes or modifies a verb. For example,

Slowly but *surely* the ship sank.

The words in *italics* are adverbs: they tell you something about *how* the ship sank — it sank *slowly* and *surely*. You can invariably (adverb) spot an adverb by its "-ly" ending.

(f) The *articles* in English are the words *the* and *a* and should present you with no problems.

(g) *Prepositions*, however, seem to present problems to everybody, especially to foreigners. Prepositions are words such as *to*, *for*, *into*, *beside*, *beneath*, *below*, *up*, *down*. For example,

   I went *into* the cupboard *beneath* the stairs.

(h) The other label you really should know is *present participle*. A *present participle* is the term we apply to that bit of the verb which ends in "-ing". For example,

   Turning and *turning* in the *widening* gyre.

The present participle conveys the idea that the action is continuing — that it is going on at this very time. But you have to be very careful: although all present participles end in "-ing", not all words which end in "-ing" are present participles. For example, the following "-ing" word *is* a present participle:

   I am walking to school at the moment

and you know this because "walking" is part of the verb "to walk". However, in this next example the "-ing" word is *not* a present participle:

   Kevin crossed at the pedestrian crossing

and you know that because "crossing" is part of the name of something — *a pedestrian crossing*. This time the "-ing" word is not part of the verb but has instead a kind of noun function. Hence, a "walking stick" is not a stick that walks, but a kind of stick for helping people to walk. Such noun-type "-ing" words we call *gerunds*.

Sentence Structure

You also need to know how sentences are structured, though in a sense we have already touched on sentence structure. You now know that English is a word-ordered language — that meaning is dependent on the order in which the words occur in a sentence. You also know that there are rules about the order — the rules allow for a certain order. For example, you can say "I am going *into the* school" but **not** "going the into school". Though these rules exist about certain word order, there is a flexibility in English which is quite astonishing. However, it is important to stress that whenever you alter the word order you also, even slightly, alter the meaning. For example,

> I know that you are clever

is slightly different in meaning from:

> That you are clever, I know.

In the second sentence attention has been drawn to the business of being clever (by putting that part of the sentence at the beginning) and the tone is more poetic: by altering both *stress* and *tone* the meaning has been correspondingly altered.

But let's take a closer look at sentence structure by examining an extract taken from *The Guardian* (and as you read it try to remember all that you have just learned):

Statistic

> And now the bloody young man is lifting a young girl from the wreckage and laying her on the verge among the roadwords. She is even bloodier than he is. You've still got one headlamp working, and that is the only light on the scene. You can see the blood quite clearly by the light of that lamp. She is writhing a bit on the verge, in an attitude of complete abandonment and indecency. Then she lies quite still and he covers her. You know she is dead. You wonder about the other car, but the young man is walking over there, and you leave it to him again. Anyway it's dark over there and you're such a coward you don't want to go and look. You excuse yourself by

thinking that as you know no first aid you could serve no useful purpose. So you stand beside what is left of your car, and you wait, and you don't really think about it at all. You are not even in any great pain anymore, but you know you've got to look at your right leg, because that's where the pain was and you use the headlight to look, and it's bloody and unreal-looking. That's *your* leg. It's always been all right in the past.

Best not look any more. That blood will just go away if you leave it. Anyway, why stand here? What to do now? If you go away, you'll just see more horrible things when they uncover whatever is in that other car. You can report the accident tomorrow. Yes, that's right. Walk home now, and report the accident tomorrow. Forget about the car. Don't want that any more. Home is 15 miles away, but it doesn't matter. Just go home, and maybe tomorrow it won't have happened. That's right, down the hill, quite easy going. Leg doesn't really mind being walked on at all. But the thrillers are wrong when they talk of *warm* blood trickling down. It isn't warm, it's cold. Everything is cold. There isn't a footpath to walk on, but it doesn't matter. Just walk in the middle of the road. Walk home. Police car pulling up? Failing to report an accident? It's an offence. You know it is. But they seem to know all about it. They want to know what car you were in, but you can't remember the number. They put you in their own car. Riding in a police car indeed. Proper Z-car, with radio. Hold the ambulance. Fifth casualty found. Leg injuries and shock. Funny they don't seem to mind that you didn't report the accident. They don't even seem to want a driving licence. Just as well. Left it at home. Then you're in the ambulance. And now you resist. Now you really resist. You're not going anywhere with that lot. Not with the girl who's dead, and the boy who's so dirty and bloody, and goodness knows what from the other car.

Look again at the first sentence of the extract:

And now the bloody young man is lifting a young girl from the wreckage and laying her on the verge among the roadworks.

Apart from the fact that the sentence starts with an "And" (and no doubt you will remember being told never to begin sentences with "and"), you will now notice the number of present participles: *lifting* and *laying*. Remember that the present participle draws attention to the continuity of the action — is that appropriate here? Go through the rest of the passage and look for other present participles, and think in terms of the effect they create. Is that effect appropriate?

We have also had a close look at verbs, and you can identify the verb in a sentence. What of the verb in the third sentence?

> You've still got one headlamp working, and that is the only light on the scene.

The first verb is "'ve" a contracted version of "have": what do you associate "You've" with — formal written English or informal spoken (or colloquial) English? Of course, it is informal, more like spoken English. Are there any other examples of such informalities?

Again, ask yourself: What is the effect of this form of the verb? What does it contribute to the overall effect of the passage? What of the sentence —

> Best not look any more.

Where is the verb? You are right — there isn't one. Again, what is the effect of this verbless sentence? Do you associate such sentences with formal written or informal spoken English? We are building up a picture of this passage, and it seems that the passage is written in a fairly colloquial style, a style which almost imitates a person's thoughts as they are going through his or her mind. Can you find any other examples of this style? What about further on:

> There isn't a footpath, but it doesn't matter. Just walk in the middle of the road. Walk home. Police car pulling up? Failing to report an accident? It's an offence. You know it is. But they seem to know all about it. They want to know what car you were in, but you can't remember the number. They put you in their own car. Riding in a police car indeed. Proper Z-car with radio. Hold the ambulance. Fifth casualty found. Leg injuries and shock. Funny they don't seem to mind that you didn't report the accident.

"Comment on the effectiveness of the sentence structure". That would be a fairly typical question in a Higher Examination Close Reading Paper: are you any more able to answer it now? What about the repetition of the pronoun plus verb? "They seem to know . . .", "They want to know . . .", "They put you in . . .": what effect do these sentences have on you? Are they what you would expect an adult to say? Look at the rest of the passage:

> Left it at home. Then you're in the ambulance. And now you resist. Now you really resist. You're not going anywhere with that lot. Not with the girl who's dead, and the boy who's so dirty and bloody, and goodness knows what from the other car.

In this section the *tone* changes. At what point does it change? How does it change? Think in terms of the effect of the repetition of "resist" and of the "and".

The repetition of the "and" is worth commenting on. Re-write that last paragraph without the "ands" and see what happens. It reads something like this:

> Now you resist. Now you really resist. You're not going anywhere with that lot. Not with the girl who's dead, the boy who's so dirty, bloody, and goodness knows what from the other car.

As you see, you can easily remove some of the "ands", but in so doing you have altered the meaning. The sentence reads more like a list now, a list which reads as though the order were haphazard.

Contrast these two sentences:

> I walked into the classroom and I saw the overturned desks, the broken chairs, the waste paper on the floor and the writing on the wall.

and

> I walked into the classroom and I saw the overturned desks and the broken chairs and the waste paper on the floor and the writing on the wall.

The difference between the two sentences, we have now learned, is one of structure: the first is in the form of a list in conventional form with the "and" between the last two items, whereas the second uses "and" between each item. The first list is in haphazard order — you can interchange the items without affecting meaning all that much, but in the second the "and" suggests that each item is linked to the one which has gone before in a significant way: "writing on the wall" takes on almost a metaphorical meaning, as though some disaster is implied, by the gradual and significant build-up. In other words, the structure with the conjunctions (polysyndetic structure) suggests or connotes something sinister in a way in which the structure without the conjunctions (asyndetic structure) does not.

One piece of advice when you are asked to comment on structure: look for any form of repetition — of a word: a conjunction, a present participle, a past participle; of a phrase; of a clause; whatever — and see what effect that repetition has. Comments about sentence structure will keep recurring in this book, which means you will keep learning about it.

Narrative Structure

"Narrative Structure" may be an unfamiliar term to you at the moment, but I think you will find that it is increasingly used or at least referred to in Revised Higher and in the course you are following at school or college. What exactly does it mean? And what relevance has it to close reading?

When you relate any story, even if what you are relating is all that happened to you from the time you got up this morning until you left the house, you would tell the story in a certain way. The least sophisticated among us would relate the events by using the "and then" narrative construction, combined no doubt, with the present tense:

> I gets out of bed and puts on my socks and then I goes through to the bathroom. I wash myself and then I goes downstairs and says "Hello" to my Mum who has my breakfast ready and then I eats it and then I goes to school.

The narrative structure here is purely chronological: it is in time sequence.

Often that is the most convenient, clearest, and most effective way of narrating events. I am talking not just about a fictional or made up story, but the narration of something that actually took place. Listen tonight to the television news: even although the presentation of the news, especially on BBC1 and ITV (or Channel 3 as it is now to be called), is very visual — with still photographs to the side of the newsreader's head and plenty of film — nevertheless he or she has to relate to you the stories that make up the day's news. Listen to how they are told: they will (must) have a narrative structure, even if that structure is a beginning, a middle, with an ending which may not be told till the story itself ends in several days time.

The simple narrative structure, then, is: *(a)* a beginning, *(b)* a middle, and *(c)* an end. Look at the story we have just read. Does it follow this simple structure? Look more closely at the beginning:

> And now the bloody young man is lifting a young girl from the wreckage and laying her on the verge among the roadworks. She is even bloodier than he is. You've still got one headlamp working, and that is the only light on the scene. You can see the blood quite clearly by the light of that lamp. She is writhing a bit on the verge, in an attitude of complete abandonment and indecency. Then she lies quite still and he covers her. You know she is dead. You wonder about the other car, but the young man is walking over there, and you leave it to him again. Anyway it's dark over there and you're such a coward you don't want to go and look.

Examine how the narrative begins: "And now the bloody young man is lifting a young girl from the wreckage and laying her on the verge among the roadworks." What does the "and now" tell us? Is this the very beginning of the story? What about "the" young man — does the "the" assume that you have met him before? (Yes, you are right, all my questions are leading ones and imply the answer!) What about the tense? Why present tense? Clearly, the story is being told after the event, so what does the writer gain from telling it in the present. You really have already answered this one earlier on when we looked at the parts of the verbs.

Now try the following exercise for yourself. Even although it is from a past Higher paper, all the questions relate to narrative structure, although such a term was not used in the early eighties!

"I'D NEVER REALLY THOUGHT OF JUDAS PRIEST AS A SAVIOUR"

When the snow finally clogged up the wipers, I knew I was in for rather more than a difficult journey.

At first, it had all seemed rather quaint and English; feathery flakes floated onto the bonnet of the car as I climbed in, and set out to cross the Pennines.

It was late, certainly, but I've always preferred night-driving, and anyway, I had a new toy to try out. A Pathfinder electronic programmable stereo radio-cassette — all advanced gadgetry and hi-tech finish — and on my own I could press buttons and twiddle knobs for the whole trip.

As I pulled onto the main road, I flicked on the radio, and almost immediately there was the announcer, warning motorists of expected heavy snowfall on high ground. Although wheel tracks were already showing black against the settling snow, and the flakes swooped over the screen like tracer bullets, I felt I'd be home and dry before the real bad stuff came down.

I recall punching the button for the BBC World Service, and hearing the comforting tones of Alistair Cooke, reading his letter from America, every word as clear as having the man in the passenger seat. The radio locked firmly onto the waveband, even among those high and craggy peaks.

As the road surface quickly turned treacherous I slotted Jackson Browne into the cassette player, and turned up the volume to concentrate my attention. The auto-reverse had played the whole thing through twice by the time I noticed that for over half an hour I'd passed no other moving vehicle. Just a couple of abandoned trucks at the foot of inclines, and a solitary car, parked forlornly at the side of a lonely phone-booth; the driver hunched over the mouthpiece, lit by the dim yellow light inside.

My progress was by now at a funeral pace. I remember thinking how apt the phrase might be, and bitterly regretting ever considering this journey. So, as I've already remarked, when the snow finally forced me to pull over, I knew I was in deep trouble.

I turned off the engine and heater, and decided to huddle down into my coat, cover myself with the picnic rug, and keep the radio on. I told myself that the news might be useful, and that in any case, the battery was now good for nothing else.

I sat and shivered for twelve long hours, at first listening to the worsening weather reports, and then playing all the tapes in the car, some (those left by my teenage son) for the first, and last, time.

Then, suddenly, I realised that something was moving, far to my right.

The drift was piled higher than the window on that side, but I could clearly hear the thump of a heavy motor. I wound the passenger window down and shouted.

I shouted 'till my throat was raw. Nothing happened. The snow muffled everything like a smothering, suffocating, pillow. The motor was now ahead of me. Soon it would be gone. And I'd still be here.

Then, a brainwave. Shuffling with numb hands among the pile of tapes, I found what I was looking for. One of my son's; 'Hero' by Judas Priest. I'd thought it remarkably powerful when I'd played it, though 'heavy metal' is hardly my thing.

But now I slotted it into the cassette player, blue fingers fumbling in their haste. I turned the volume up full, pushed the tape firmly in, and covered my ears with my hands. The bass reverberated round the whole car, the Pathfinder cross-axial speakers on the rear parcel shelf practically took off, and even with covered ears I marvelled at the pitch of the lead singer's howl . . .

The snowplough men told me that they'd been a shade scared at first by the banshee wail issuing from an apparently empty landscape, but had quickly caught on.

They'd got to me before the tape finished, and just as the car battery gave out.

I suppose I ought to drop a line to Judas Priest, whoever he, or they, might be.

Although it was really my Pathfinder that saved my life.

PATHFINDER
THE PERFECT TRAVELLING COMPANION

Marks

(a) Although the pasage is obviously an advertisement for Pathfinder radio-cassette players, the text is in the form of a short story—there is a narrative line.

    (i) Examine carefully the first paragraph and say why it is effective as an opening to a short story.   1

    (ii) How does the author use the weather as an important element throughout the story?   2

    (iii) In what two ways does the author indicate a time-lapse after "singer's howl"?   2

    (iv) Important to this story is the character of the person supposed to be telling it. Explain by means of an example how the author creates a character who appears real to the reader.   2

    (v) By referring to two examples, show how the author demonstrates the features of Pathfinder cassette players within the context of the story.   4

(b) Much of the humour in the text is a slightly mocking tongue-in-cheek play on words. Quote and comment on any two examples of this kind of humour.   4

Total for Question (15)

It is important to know about narrative structure when it comes to close reading in that you might well be asked questions about it. But, in a sense more importantly, you should know about it because an understanding of narrative structure will enable you to grasp more quickly all kinds of aspects of the passage you are studying, and of literature in general since, as I have said, all stories must have a narrative structure. We shall return to this idea when we come to look at the critical essay.

So far we have looked at grammar, sentence structure and narrative structure. You have to have an understanding of these matters in order to be able to tackle the interpretation passage (or any other passage or book, for that matter). You also need to know about punctuation and word-choice to be fully equipped for all that might arise.

Punctuation

There are no absolute rules about punctuation, only certain conventions governing the ways in which we use punctuation marks. These conventions change over the years and occasionally some writers quite deliberately break the generally accepted conventions of the written language to create a specific effect.

The comma is used less frequently nowadays than formerly. In business letters, for example, punctuation marks tend to be omitted from the address, from the salutation at the beginning of the letter and from the subscription.

Commas are used to clarify the text and to avoid ambiguity. For example:

> This number is being played live in response to many requests by Simple Minds.

The uncertainty and ambiguity in the above sentence is removed by the addition of commas:

> This number is being played live, in response to many requests, by Simple Minds.

Commas are also used to separate items in a list, to indicate apposition and to indicate any interruption in the flow of a sentence. Often, though, the decision whether or not to use a comma is a matter of taste rather than rule.

The semi-colon may be used to indicate an interconnection between items which in themselves could stand as grammatically independent statements. It is more frequently used to separate items in a complex list where commas are already used.

The colon has a variety of valuable uses: it often indicates that an example or illustration or expansion of the words before it is about to appear. It may well contribute to the balance of a sentence which contains contrasting ideas. For example:

> To err is human: to forgive divine.

It can also be used to introduce a quotation or a list.

The paired dash and *paired brackets* are used to isolate information which is additional to the text but separate from it. For example:

> I often go to the disco — the one off Union Street — on Friday evenings.

or
> I met Kevin at the disco last night. (He often goes there on Fridays. He says the atmosphere is better there.) He told me about the strangest happening.

The single dash is often used to indicate an afterthought, or, more recently, to replace the colon or semi-colon.

Inverted commas are used to indicate the words actually used by a speaker in direct speech; the words of a quotation; titles of books, plays, films, etcetera; or to indicate a word used in an unusual way or slightly out of context.

The apostrophe has two separate functions: to denote the contraction of a word by the omission of a letter or letters (such as 'don't' or 'can't') and to indicate possession.

The forming of the possessive noun in the singular is really very straightforward: you take the noun as it stands, add an apostrophe, and then add an 's'. For example:

    man   — the man's chair
    fox   — the fox's lair
    lady   — the lady's book
    James   — St. James's Park

If, however, the above rule leads to a pronunciation difficulty 's' need not be added. For example, we say "Moses' sisters" rather than "Moses's sisters".

The forming of the possessive noun in the plural is a little more complicated, but it shouldn't really create the difficulties that often occur in candidates' writing. Take the plural form of the noun as it stands — dogs, children, candidates, men, asses. Next look carefully at the ending of the word: if it does **not** end in an 's' then treat the word as you do for the singular noun — add an apostrophe then an 's':

    children   — children's toys
    men   — men's clothes
    women   — women's scarves.

If the noun ends in 's' in the plural, add an apostrophe but do **not** add an 's':

    foxes   — the foxes' lair
    asses   — the asses' heads
    ladies   — the ladies' waiting-room.

If you are still not sure what to do, then rather than add apostrophes in the most ridiculous of places, the wisest procedure is just to omit them altogether. Little looks more illiterate than the apostrophe in the wrong place, whereas an apostrophe omitted looks like modern practice.

There are other kinds of punctuation marks (such as underlining, *italics*, **bold letters**, BLOCK CAPITALS) sometimes referred to as typographical devices. Remember that the function of punctuation is to make meaning clear, to make the reader's job easier, to avoid confusion and ambiguity. If you are asked a question about a particular piece of punctuation, ask yourself *how* it is supporting meaning, what difference would it make to omit the mark? The answer to these questions will provide you with a basis for your answer to the question in the exam paper.

The Close Reading Passage

This is perhaps the bit of the Higher paper that candidates dread most. Yet, in fact, it is not all that badly done, and the evidence from candidates' performances over the years suggest that there are other bits of the paper less well done than Paper II Part 1.

The best adivce I can give you is to tell you to read as much as you can throughout your Higher year, especially anything from a quality newspaper such as *The Guardian*, *The Independent* or *Scotland on Sunday*. The more familiar you are with the kind of prose that is in newspapers such as these, the less strange will seem the kind of prose you will meet in the exam itself.

When it comes to answering the questions, don't waste time by writing too much or by spending a disproportionate amount of time on any one question. After each question you will see the number of marks in brackets: this is a good guide to the amount you are expected to write. For example, a 2-mark question probably requires two points to be made whereas a 4-mark question suggests that there are four points to be made. Most certainly, if you make only one point in answer to a 4-mark question, the chances are very high that you will score no more than one mark.

You cannot really benefit by practising "doing" interpretation, no matter what people tell you. What you have to improve are your reading skills, and you will improve them only by reading as much as you can.

What can be helpful is to be able to recognise the kind of questions that are likely to come up each year so that you will have some idea about how to answer them for example, it does not matter that you can answer a particular question in a particular year about a particular image, but what does matter is that you know what an image is and how to answer questions concerning images.

You need to be able to recognise questions about meaning, and how to answer them; questions that explore the ideas of any given passage, and how to answer them; questions about linkage within a passage, and how to answer them; questions about sentence structure and word choice, and how to answer them, and questions that ask you to compare aspects of prose, and how to answer them.

Questions about Meaning

Generally questions about meaning occur at the beginning of the set of questions and are fairly straightforward. The passage will be of moderate difficulty and you will be expected to know the meanings of fairly difficult words. If you don't know the meaning of a particular word, don't give up, but try to work it out from the rest of the passage. Use your common sense.

Questions which Explore the Ideas of a Passage

Such questions tend to follow the questions about the meaning of words and again they are not difficult to answer. In fact, one of the easy things about questions concerning ideas is that the answer to them must necessarily lie in the passage: go to the area of text being questioned (often you are directed to the area by the question itself), examine carefully the relevant bit, put it into your own words, and then write down your answer noting carefully the number of marks since they will be a guide to the number of points required

Questions about Linkage

In many ways questions about linkage are a gift, and yet so many candidates fail to be able to do them. Set about these questions this way:

    (a)   read carefully the link sentence to which you have been directed by the question;

(b) look at the first few words of the sentence: work out to which preceding words or ideas they refer;

(c) look at the remainder of the link sentence: work out which words in this part of the sentence refer to ideas still to come;

(d) now you are ready to answer: *quote* the actual words from the beginning of the link sentence and show to which actual ideas or words they refer, and then *quote* the words from the end of the sentence and show to which actual ideas these words refer.

You must quote and show how the words quoted do the job of linking. Usually these questions are marked as follows: ½ mark for words quoted + ½ mark for demonstrating the link *back to the previous paragraph(s)* plus ½ mark for words quoted + ½ mark *for demonstrating the link forwards*. Thus, the sentence (I know the example is contrived when out of context like thus, but it will do):

All this might be excusable if the BBC had plenty of money to spare.

acts as a link because "All this" refers back to the ideas of the BBC's overspending of its funds (in any case, "this" is a demonstrative adjective which must have an antecedent in the previous paragraph) and "if the BBC had plenty of money to spare" (the "if" suggests that it hasn't) anticipates the ideas of shortages which the writer is about to explore.

Questions about Sentence Structure

We have already dealt with sentence structure on pages 34 – 38. What you really want to establish is how the sentence structure contributes to the meaning. Always refer closely to the text in your answer to questions about sentence structure and, indeed, quote the actual bits of structure to which you are referring.

Questions about Word-choice

Questions about word-choice are generally questions about the appropriateness (or otherwise) of the words the author has chosen. It is helpful for you to understand the difference between the denotative and the connotative area of a word: the denotative area of a word is the object in the universe to which the word refers. If I say that I am sitting at my desk writing this book and the sun is shining, the denotation of "desk" is the actual desk at which I am writing, the denotation of "sun" is the actual sun, which, believe it or not, is actually and denotatively shining right now. The connotation of a word is the picture conjured up in our minds by our associations with that particular word and our experiences of it. For example, the word "fall" could suggest anything from the idea of a stumble over a bumpy pavement, through the notion of autumn to the concept of man's fall from grace and his expulsion from the Garden of Eden, each picture depending on the person's associations of the word.

What, then, are the connotations of "the sun is shining" if someone says: "The sun is shining for me today"? And remember, don't give the meaning of the phrase, say what the associations, the word pictures, are for you.

These associations are the connotation of the word, and a writer will use a word in order to exploit its connotative area. The skilful reader is sensitive to this connotative area (as well as to the meaning of the word) and is able to work out whether or not the writer's choice of that particular word is appropriate and, therefore, effective. You are unlikely to be asked for the connotative area of a word (how could you be wrong?), but you will be asked about the effectiveness of a writer's word-choice. In order to talk about a word's effectiveness, you really have to explore the connotative area first of all and then show how that area is in keeping with what the writer wants to say. For example, if you were asked about the effectiveness of the word-choice in the line from *Macbeth*:

> His secret murders sticking on his hands

you would want to talk about "secret" and "sticking". Are these words effective? Well, think of what the word "secret" suggests to you: is that suggestion in keeping with the idea of murder, particularly the murder of King Duncan? What of "sticking"? Again, what is suggested to you by the word? Is it in keeping with the state of mind that Macbeth is in at this point in the play? Is it, therefore, appropriate?

Questions which Ask You to Make Comparisons

In Paper I Part 1, you can be given two passages, as was the case in 1989 and 1990. If the two passages are related, as they were in both these years, you could be asked to make some kind of comparison of them in terms of either content or language or both. Candidates find this kind of question difficult, which is a pity since often it attracts fairly high marks. All you have to do is to remember the advice I have given you: whenever you make a point about the text, you must support that point by close reference to the text. You might, for example, want to say that passage A is humorous, whereas passage B is very serious: those comments are very general and really say nothing until you support them by illustrating passage A's humour with a reference by illustrating passage B's seriousness by a reference. A comment plus supporting quotation usually earns 1 mark + 1 mark.

This has been a long chapter, and it contains a great deal of information. You will need to read and re-read it, and probably make your own notes from it. In fact, it is a splendid idea for you to make your own notes in that special notebook I asked you to buy, and for you also to record examples of the various language features we have been talking about as you come across them. I find that a superb source of material which uses unusual language features is the advertising you find in colour supplements and even on billboards. The people who make up advertisements are only too aware of language techniques — maybe as aware of them as poets are — and therefore advertisements are well worth paying attention to — linguistically speaking, of course. Cut out the better examples and keep them in that section of your notebook which deals with language and the way it works.

All that has been said here about interpretation applies just as much to Practical Criticism, which is the subject of the next chapter.

Chapter III

PRACTICAL CRITICISM

Paper I, Part 2, Section A, according to the Revised Arrangements document, will "contain a previously unseen poem, piece of prose, or dramatic dialogue with associated questions".

For some bizarre reason, few teachers and even fewer candidates like Practical Criticism. Teachers suggest to candidates that PC is "difficult" and should be attempted only by the very clever; this is patently not true. The correlation between candidates' performance in essay-type questions and PC is very high indeed.

Apart from the fact that the statistics prove that some teachers and some candidates are wrong in thinking PC is too difficult, the advice that candidates should avoid it is equally erroneous: quite simply, it cannot be avoided. In Revised Higher, many of the interpretation questions are Practical Criticism-type questions, and the interpretation is compulsory.

In any case, the technique for studying literature by examining theme, character, situation, narrative structure in terms of how these things are established and developed is Practical Criticism: look back at what I said in Chapter I of this book, and look closely at *The Practical Guide to Literature* and *The Practical Guide to Poetry* (1990). Each of these books deals with the study of literature and each of them stresses the importance of the technique of Practical Criticism.

What is Practical Criticism? Well, I have really answered that question already. It is, on the one hand, a technique for studying literature. Remember the three questions?

(a) What is the text about? [answer in themes]
(b) What effects does it have on me? [I laugh, cry, etc.]
(c) How have these effects been produced? [author technique]

The last of these questions *(c)* is Practical Criticism: an examination of author technique and the effect of language features.

Practical Criticism is also a technique for examining literature whereby the candidate is asked questions about technique and the use of language features.

You must read again the previous chapter because everything you need to know for the interpretation paper about language and the way it works, you also need to know for Practical Criticism. What you also must remember is that the skills for PC are not skills that you can acquire in a term: they are skills that need to have been developed over five years of secondary education; the continued close reading study of texts, as suggested above and elsewhere, however, will help to develop and sharpen those skills.

What might be useful for you to know, however, is that there is a kind of pattern to the set of questions that appear in the Practical Criticism in this paper. The first few questions, for example, are always quite easy: this is a deliberate policy on the part of the examiners in order *(a)* to relax you and to help you come to terms with the question, and *(b)* in order to ensure a parity with the Specified Text questions, the first few questions of which are also relatively straightforward.

These easier questions are invariably set to establish the situation and the mood. "Situation" always seems within the grasp of most candidates, but "mood" seems to create problems. It shouldn't: think in terms of the second question — "What effects does it have on me?". Mood is about the feeling created in you by the passage, and all you have to do is to say *how* that mood has been created. Let us take an example. Read carefully the following poem:

THEIR LONELY BETTERS

As I listened from a beach-chair in the shade
To all the noises that my garden made,
It seemed only proper that words
Should be withheld from vegetables and birds.

A robin with no Christian name ran through
A Robin-Anthem which was all it knew,
And rustling flowers for some third party waited
To say which pairs, if any, should get mated.

No one of them was capable of lying,
There was not one which knew that it was dying
Or could have with a rhythm or a rhyme
Assumed responsibility for time.

Let them leave language to their lonely betters
Who count some days and long for certain letters;
We, too, make noises when we laugh or weep:
Words are for those with promises to keep.

                                                         W.H. Auden

Once you have read the poem two or three times, you should have some idea of the situation in the poem and of who is speaking. The poet (or, more accurately, the persona created by the poet) is speaking, and he seems to be sitting in his garden in a beach-chair, and the seat is in the shade. That is perfectly straightforward, isn't it?

Now what is the mood? In a very general sense, ask yourself what mood is created by a picture of someone sitting in his or her garden in the shade? (Quite a different mood from one suggested by someone looking out of a window into the rain-soaked darkly lit street, I suspect.) You think a relaxed mood? Unhurried? Reflective? Contemplative? Of course you are right. Now what you must do is look closely at the actual words used and say how — even simply in terms of their meaning — they contribute to this mood. For example, the poet (or persona) is listening to the "noises" his garden made. The poet has chosen to use the word "noises" rather than, say, "sounds". Of course there is a difference in meaning; but there is also a difference in connotation. "Noises" suggests meaningless sound, almost unpleasantly disturbing.

But please do not stop at the words — after all, there is more to a poem than merely words. Remember that a most important aspect of poetry is *sound* and sound in a poem is created by rhyme as well as word-choice.

So, how does rhyme in this poem help to contribute to the mood on which we are agreed? Think, first of all, in terms of vowel sounds. Notice the idle and relaxed effect of the long vowel sounds in "shade" and "made", and the reinforcement of that effect by the poet's use of rhyme, which draws attention to the sound. The effect is further reinforced by the para-rhyme of "words" and "birds". (Para-rhyme is a rhyme which is not quite a rhyme: unlike "shade" and "made", which is a perfect rhyme, "birds" does not have exactly the same sound as "words", though it is very close.)

You should also examine sentence structure to see what contribution it makes to effect: and here, in verse one, you cannot help but note that the verse is all one sentence, helping to create a mood of idleness and relaxation by its very length. What about:

> It seemed only proper that words
> Should be withheld . . . . ?

What does the order "seemed only proper" and "should be withheld" suggest? Isn't there a slightly superior attitude suggested by the word-choice and structure? He doesn't write: "Vegetables and birds are not able to speak" but that the power of words has somehow been deliberately withheld from them and that this act is also "proper".

Do you see how I am examining very closely the actual language used by the poet to see what subtle shades of meaning I can elicit?

I have spent a long time on situation and mood, and that is because I think it is very important to be able to establish the situation and mood at the beginning not only of a poem, but of any work be it literature, film or television. It is also because most Practical Criticism exercises begin with questions on these.

The questions in a PC exercise get progressively more difficult. Again this is a deliberate policy by the examiners; after all, this section of the paper must test the most able candidates as well as everybody else.

One thing to bear in mind, however, is that the questions always relate to language and how it is used to create effect. If you look at what I have done above, although my analysis is related to situation and mood, nevertheless the way I go about it — the examination of language — applies to other aspects you might be questioned about. For example, let's take a typical practical criticism question concerning the poem we have been dealing with:

> Trace the ways in which the distinction between "noises" (line 2) and "words" (line 3) is continued and developed in the remainder of the poem. (6 marks)

Now what you must note initially is the number of marks — in this case 6. That is quite a number and you are going to have to do a fair amount of work to earn all the marks. But when you look at the question you can see that there is quite a lot to do anyway: you have to trace the ways in which a distinction is continued and developed.

In PC it is often very difficult, sometimes impossible, to earn marks unless you make clear references to the passage. You cannot really answer this question without references. What, then, are the references to words and what are the references to noises? Look at the *whole* poem:

> "Christian name", "Robin-anthem", "rustling", "to say", "lying", "rhyme", "language", "count", "letters", "noises", "laugh", "weep", "words", "promises".

If all that you do is to make one reference from each of the three remaining stanzas without any comment at all, you will earn 3 marks! That alone should indicate to you the tremendous importance of making close reference to the text in PC. However, let us see what distinction we can trace when we examine these words: firstly "words" seem to be linked to the notion of self-awareness or of knowledge of one's own identity, to knowledge of death, to awareness of time passing, to the ability to lie, whereas "noises" seem to be linked to the inability to make choices or decisions, the inability to lie, the inability to deceive or be insincere, the ignorance of time or death. I have done a very thorough job, trying to include *all* that I get from the words and ideas. Were you to select any one of these notions and relate it clearly and unambiguously to the language used, you would have done enough to earn full marks.

The point I am trying to make is that, once you know what is expected of you, it is really quite easy to do well in Practical Criticism: you *must* always make reference to the text and you must always support any comments you make by such references — just as I have done.

You must bear in mind the fact that you are examining language and how it is used.

Chapter IV

SPECIFIED TEXTS

Paper I, Part 2, Section B, according to the Revised Arrangements document, will contain a key passage from each of the specified prose or dramatic texts. It will also contain a complete poem, or a key passage from a poem, from each of the specified sets of poems. Each passage and poem will be accompanied by its own set of associated questions. Candidates choosing Section B will attempt the questions on *one* of these key passages or poems. The questions will test candidates' knowledge of the passage, its immediate context and its relationship to the text as a whole. For poetry, questions will also test awareness of relationships with other poem(s) in the specified set.

In the first instance, these texts will be set for a period of not less than three years. Thereafter, one or more than one of the specified texts/sets will be changed, with one year's notice of change being given.

At least two of the texts, according to the document, will be by Scottish writers. Non-fiction will be represented periodically.

The list for 1991 will be exactly the same as the list for 1990; the changes to the list, *for 1992 only*, are minimal: *Romeo and Juliet* instead of *Macbeth*, and *Sunset Song* instead of *Greenvoe*.

There are, then, nine set texts/sets of poems from which to choose. And here I give you a fairly strong piece of advice:

    (a) prepare no more than *two* specified texts for Section B;

    (b) do *not* use specified texts anywhere else in the examination especially in Paper II for your answer to the literature question.

We need to go back to what the Arrangements document actually says:

> The questions will test candidates' knowledge of the passage, its immediate context and its relationship to the text as a whole. For poetry, questions will also test awareness of relationships with other poem(s) in the specified set.

All of which means that you can expect at least three sets of questions, the first of which will concern the extract (or poem) itself, the second of which will deal with the relationship of the extract to its immediate context, and the third of which will deal with the ways in which the passage or extract relates to the work as a whole. We shall now take each of these questions in turn.

Questions which test knowledge of the passage

The examiners do not want such questions to be purely recall questions that test little else but memory, though clearly you will be expected to know whereabouts in the novel, play, or poem the passage occurs. You need not be able to remember precise details, but you are, after all, expected to have a working knowledge of the text. You can, then, anticipate a question that will draw on your knowledge and understanding of the ideas, themes, characters in the extract itself. An example will make things clearer. In the 1989 Higher, Paper I, Part 1, Section B, Question 4 (*Wuthering Heights*) you will find the following context question:

(a) (i) Who is the narrator and who is the listener in this extract?

(ii) Explain briefly what effect the method of narration in the novel has on the way you view the characters in this scene.

The fact that you are asked who's who in the first question does not belie what I said about recall questions: you can hardly read *Wuthering Heights* and *not* know who is who. The question should earn you an easy mark. The second question exemplifies what I have been saying about testing your knowledge and understanding of what is going on in the extract itself. On this occasion you are being asked about character and the method of narration.

But do you see how well you are expected to know the text? Not only do you need to know about the method of narration — in this novel, or in any other novel — but you need to know how that method of narration has affected the way you view the characters. Now it is only too easy to say that the novel is told through the eyes of So-and-so, or even to be able to use the technical jargon of First Person Narration, but it is much more difficult to say *how* the particular method has affected *your* understanding of theme or character or whatever. It is the experience of the examiners that in fact most candidates cannot say how a method of narration affects their understanding. Yet, if you think about it, the answer is easy. The problem is that you probably haven't given the matter enough thought: you know *what* the method of narration is but not *how* it affects the reader who, in this case, is the all-important you.

Think about exactly who is the narrator, what age and kind of person he/she is, what sorts of experiences he/she has been through, what are his/her preoccupations, interests, prejudices, etcetera; then, since that person is a filter through which you view the events and other characters in the novel, think in terms of how that person's character *must* affect his/her view of things and, therefore, ultimately your view of things. This is the kind of thinking you should do long before the examination in May, and, indeed, the results of such thinking should be jotted in your notebook since they will form an integral and vital part of your notes.

Here is the next question in the same Paper:

> *(b)* Comment, in detail, referring to the language used, on the way Catherine greets the dogs and the people after her five week absence. (6 marks)

Again you will note that, although this follows as a separate question, it is still a question based on the extract, although your answer would inevitably have to draw on your knowledge and understanding of the novel itself. You are asked in this question to refer to the language used, and you can be absolutely certain that failure to do so will lead to failure itself: you must, as always, make close reference to the text.

Questions which deal with the relationship of the passage to its immediate context

The following is the next question, again in the *Wuthering Heights* passage, in the same Paper:

> The critic E.M. Forster commented, "The emotions of Heathcliff and Catherine surround them like thunderclouds and generate the explosions that fill the novel."
>
> (i) Explain in detail what you think are the causes of the "explosion" in this scene. (4 marks)
>
> (ii) Give a brief account of any other scene from the novel, showing how it further illustrates the truth of Forster's statement. (4 marks)

The number of marks available (shown here in brackets at the end of each question) is an important guide to the amount you are required to write. You can see right away that these questions move your thinking on a bit: you are being taken outside the extract. It is quite impossible to answer these questions without having studied and thoroughly understood the novel. (i) asks you about the causes of the explosion, and clearly these causes have their origin in events and attitudes before this extract begins, and (ii) asks you to show how another scene from the novel illustrates Forster's contention that the "explosions" are generated by the emotions of Heathcliff and Catherine: you need to have a sound and thorough working knowledge of the novel to be able to deal with a question such as this.

Questions which deal with the relationship of the passage to the work as a whole

The final kind of question (or questions) that you will be asked are those which deal with the relationship of the extract to the work as a whole, or, if the passage is a poem, to another poem or other poems in the same set of specified poems. Let's look at the next question from the same Paper (1989):

> (d) By making close reference to at least *two* scenes, show how the details of setting help you understand better the ideas of this novel.

You can see immediately that this is a much more general kind of question in that you need to know about themes and setting, but, unlike a conventional literature question, you are asked to relate the setting to the themes by making close reference to two scenes: in other words, although this appears to be a general question, it actually demands very specific detailed knowledge of the text.

Don't be fooled into thinking that this is an easy kind of question: you really do need to know the specified texts in detail and you need to be able to refer to very specific areas of them. But what I want to stress above all is that you must be able to select from your comprehensive knowledge of the text the areas relevant to the question asked. What the examiners have found is that no matter what question is asked candidates are determined to put down everything they know: they fire their knowledge like grapeshot from a blunderbuss at the question, hoping (against hope) that some of the pellets of knowledge will hit the right bits of the question.

Such a method will inevitably lead to failure. You have to be able to select from your knowledge. In this case, you must have an idea before you tackle the question of how aspects of setting help the reader to understand the ideas of the novel, and then you must select from your knowledge of the novel as a whole those scenes that will best illustrate the points you want to make. You must stick to what it is the question asks and you must resist the temptation to put down things just because you know them.

I said right at the beginning of this chapter that you should prepare no more than two specified texts: in fact, there is really no need to prepare more than one. There are very good reasons for giving you this advice, the most important of which is that you can really only prepare one, at the most two, texts in sufficient detail to be able to deal with them satisfactorily in the examination. Another important reason is that if you spend too much time and energy preparing three or more texts for this section of the examination, you will have neither the time nor the energy to prepare properly a sufficient number of other literary texts for Paper II.

"So what?" you might quip. "I can always use in Paper II whatever specified text I did not use in Paper I!"

My reply is quite simple: Please don't. I'll explain why later. In the meantime, simply trust me when I tell you not to use a specified text in Paper II, and that therefore you shouldn't waste time preparing too many for Paper I.

In the 1990 Paper I, Part 2, Section B, Number 1 — Keats — there are only *four* questions. In fact, if you look at all of the specified text passages you will see that none of the the associated sets of questions is more than four in number, with the exception of *Death of a Salesman*, which has five. You will also notice that in all of them the last question is worth 10 marks. I am not commenting, merely pointing to a fact, as George Orwell once claimed in another context.

In each case, these four questions (five in *Death of a Salesman*) still concern themselves with the three areas previously outlined: questions which test your knowledge of the passage itself, questions which explore the relationship of the passage to its immediate context, and questions which explore the relationship of the passage to the work as a whole (or, in the case of poetry, to another poem or other poems). Even if, in future years, the number of questions attached to each set text is increased, they will still concern themselves with these three areas.

Let us return to the questions on Keats. The passage is taken from the beginning of *Ode to Autumn*, the first two stanzas, in fact. Again the first two questions are to do with the first of the areas outlined above — questions which test your knowledge of the passage itself:

(a) Who is being addressed as "thee" in line 12? (1 mark)

(b) Comment in detail on how the poet makes you aware of fruitfulness or ripeness throughout stanza 1. (8 marks)

Both these questions are to do with the passage itself, but both also demand a previous knowledge of the poem. In other words, it would be difficult to answer these questions if you had not studied the poem beforehand. Although question *(b)* is a bit like a practical criticism-type question, you would have to spend a lot longer in working out the answer to it if you had not already considered the techniques the poet adopts. Remember that this question is worth 8 marks, and that, since the number of marks is a guide to the length of answer required, you are expected in this case to answer in considerable detail. You need to be able to draw on knowledge and understanding developed prior to your sitting the examination, since you have not time in the exam itself to work things out from first principles.

The next question is about the relationship of the passage with the immediate context:

(c) Keats wrote in a letter:

"I never lik'd stubble fields so much as now — Aye better than the chilly greeen of spring. Somehow a stubble plain looks warm — in the same way that some pictures look warm."

Show how the poet develops autumn as "warm" by considering the effectiveness of three images or "pictures" from the poem as a whole.   (6 marks)

Since we are dealing here with poetry, the "immediate context" can be, and in this case is, the whole poem. You can see, once again, that your knowledge and understanding of the poem needs to be detailed and thorough in order for you to answer this question. In order to earn all 6 marks, you have to deal with three images — which means, of course, you have to be able to refer to three such images from your studies of the poem (see how well you have to know it?). You need to be able to identify very clearly the images you are going to discuss, and you need to be able to refer to them in close detail as you discuss their effectiveness in portraying autumn as warm.

Although there are 6 marks available for this question and although there are three images to be discussed, that does not mean that it will be marked mechanically by awarding two marks to each image: it is not marked 2 + 2 + 2! If you give a very full discussion of one image that might earn you more than two marks, but, as I have already pointed out, in order to earn all six marks you have to deal with three images.

How do you go about answering a question such as this? Well, you'll notice that it is the type of practical criticism question that could well turn up in the interpretation(s) or, of course, in the PC itself: it is a question about writer technique — about how an image has been created and about how effectively this has been done. The way to answer it is the same as the way you would answer any such question: firstly, identify the image, then examine carefully the language to show how the image is portrayed — in so doing, be sure to make clear how effective you consider it to be. For example "maturing sun" is obviously a "warm" image — that's the image identified — now go on to show how "maturing sun" helps the author convey autumn as warm. Bear in mind that the "close bosom-friend" of the "maturing sun" is the "season of mists and mellow fruitfulness" and that this season conspires with the sun to "load and bless / With fruit the vines that round the thatch-eaves run". The idea of the maturing sun, that is, a sun which is mature (because it is in its autumn) and which thereby helps other things mature, conspiring with autumn not only to help ripen the grapes but to afford them blessing is an idea which suggests warmth in all senses of that word.

You see what I have been doing? It is exactly what you must do every time you are asked a similar kind of question. Firstly, identify the image, then make close reference to the text in order to support what you want to say about the image, and, finally, show *how* the language is used to convey the connotations of the image. It is so important to make a reference to the text and then to make a comment about the reference. Put very simply, what you do is: Quote + Comment.

What I have written above is sufficient to earn me at least 2 marks, though I have to remember that I have to repeat the procedure for two other images, and I have to refer to areas of the poem not in the passage. It is not really all that difficult.

The final question *(d)* is about the relationship of this poem to one other by Keats:

> *(d)* The poet's use of sound throughout *Ode to Autumn*, and in the third stanza particularly, is striking. Referring to this poem, and to another by Keats, show how the use of sound has made them memorable for you. (10 marks)

Again, the very first thing to note is that there are all of 10 marks available — a lot of marks! You really have to do a lot to earn them all. And I would start with a plan. Your answer is obviously going to have to be quite long and sustained, and, in order to achieve both length and substance, you are going to have to produce a plan. There is nothing mysterious about such a plan: you need an introductory paragraph in which you outline the points you are going to make, followed by a development of each of the points such that you are building up a case or argument, and finally you need a conclusion in which you draw together the strands of your argument, but in which you say nothing new. In effect, this answer is almost a mini critical essay, the bigger brother of which you will have to produce in Paper II.

In fact, if you look at each of the specified text questions, you will find that without exception the last question is worth 10 marks, and again you can assume that such an arrangement is deliberate. Clearly the idea of going beyond the passage into other areas of the text, or to other poem(s) is an important part of this kind of assessment, and the marks allocated have to reflect that fact. Also, if, in each of the texts, a similar kind of question is given the same number of marks, then the fairness of the examination is maintained: it would be quite wrong to have such a question worth 5 marks for one specified text and 12 marks for another.

In conclusion, then, remember the advice I gave you at the outset: prepare no more than two specified texts (and if you prepare two, make one a set of poems), and make sure you have a sound knowledge of the texts you have chosen as well as a thorough understanding of the ideas, issues and themes it contains. Know how character is established, how the setting is created and how all these things relate to each other.

Whatever else, if there is a specified text you have prepared but not used in Paper I, please do not use that text as a basis for your answer to the Critical Essay in Paper II. The rules of the examination are set out in Appendix 2 for handy reference.

Chapter V

REPORT OR FORMAL ESSAY

The Revised Arragements Document details on page 20 of the current edition the arrangements for Paper II.

Firstly, there is a Report:

> The report is a test of writing skills involving analysis, evaluation, selection and sequencing of material provided.
>
> Candidates will be required to study several related texts, analyse and evaluate the information they contain, select what is relevant to the assignment set, and produce a report which reorganises the material into a coherent piece of continuous formal prose of appropriate length. A suggested length will be indicated in the rubric and will normally be within the range of 300 – 400 words. The report will not involve role-play but will require consistency of stance and tone.

Secondly, there is the Critical Essay:

> Candidates will be required to write a critical essay of approximately 500 words in continuous formal prose on *one* of a choice of topics.
>
> There will be a number of literary topics arranged in three sections: Section A — Drama; Section B — Prose; Section C — Poetry. At least one question will always be concerned with Shakespearean drama. Works in translation, where appropriate, may be used. There will also be a number of topics relating to the mass media in a further section — Section D. The mass media topics will deal with each of the specified areas of study as well as offering more general questions.
>
> In all four sections it will be possible for a candidate to choose a Scottish text or texts as the basis for an answer.

The specified areas of study of the mass media for 1991 (and 1992) will be:

    Film;   Narrative;   Representations.

In the first instance these areas of study will be set for a period of not less than three years. Thereafter, one or more than one of the specified areas will be changed, with one year's notice of change being given.

Revised Arrangements document then goes on to deal with the restrictions on this part of the paper: you cannot use for your Critical Essay any text that you have already used in the RPR or in Paper I; moreover, if you have answered a Specified Text in Paper I, then you must choose a different genre of text for your answer in this paper. Don't worry, I'll deal with these restrictions in such detail later that you will be in no doubt about what you can and cannot do.

Back to Part 1 of Paper II: The Report. Actually, if you look carefully at all the examination Paper IIs, you will see that the word "report" is not used. The examiners prefer to use the term "formal essay". I said right at the beginning of this book that one of the distinguishing features of this Higher is its emphasis on discursive writing: if you think about it, the RPR requires you to write discursively in formal continuous prose; you have an opportunity to write in discursive prose (if you so wish) in the writing part of your Personal Studies Folio (see page 5 of this book); and you are required to write discursively and formally in this part of Paper II and in the Critical Essay as well. That adds up to a great deal of discursive writing, which means it would be silly to ignore it as a skill.

You may rightly ask: what is meant by discursive writing? We tell you in school that there are three kinds of writing — creative writing, personal writing and discursive writing. Discursive writing is the kind of writing that you are most likely to use after you have left school, and so it makes sense that a Higher in English should present you with plenty of opportunities to display your skills in it.

Discursive writing is the style of writing someone uses when he or she wants to deploy or set out ideas. I have already dealt fairly fully with discursive writing in the first Chapter of this book (see pages 26 – 27) and there is little point in repeating it all again, but there is a difference between writing discursively on a subject of your own choice and writing discursively in this Paper: the difference is that here you have no choice!

When you decide to write discursively about an issue of your own choosing, the first task you have to undertake is you have to research the material. If you want to write about, say, the destruction of the Amazonian rainforest, then you have to find out where the forest is exactly, what it is, and why its destruction is important or significant. You have to evaluate that material, deciding what is relevant for the argument you want to construct. You may come across information that is conflicting or counter-arguments of which you had not originally thought. All, you may feel, ought to be dealt with to show the thoroughness of your research and the strength of your argument. Then you have to present your material in an attractive and meaningful way to a reader who may know much less than you and who may have little interest.

In this part of the Paper you have to do no research whatever — it has been done for you by a painstaking and thankless examiner. You will be presented with the researched material, and the first thing you will have to do is to read and study it carefully. Once you have done that, look again at the first paragraph. The following first paragraph is taken from the 1990 paper:

> Read the various items which follow, and then, when you have decided your own viewpoint, write an essay for people who might have a general interest in the argument. The essay should convey your view, taking into account the points made in these items. You must base your conclusion entirely on the material presented to you, and on any direct inferences you can draw from it.

There are various aspects of these instructions to which I want to draw your attention. The instructions tell you to:

> *write an essay for people who might have a general interest in the argument.*

The first thing to note is that you are not given a *specific* task or remit — you are simply asked to write an essay. This is a clear indication that what is wanted in a discursive essay based on the information given. But since you have not been given a task, you really have to set yourself one. That does not mean you have to invent some silly role for yourself: a careful reading of the material should make clear for you what the task should be. The information given will contain contentious material — that is, built into the material will be some kind of conflict or opposing views. Your job is to present that conflict to the general reader in such a way that the conflict is made clear as is the side of the argument with which you agree.

I have just mentioned "the general reader", and I worked that out from that bit of the instruction which says that you have to write this essay "for people who might have a general interest in the argument". This is a clear statement of the audience for whom you are writing: the educated person who has no specialised knowledge. The style or tone that you should adopt, then, is that of formal, continuous prose. You are *not* being asked to be persuasive or argumentative or hectoring; you are not being asked to write in a style to which you are not accustomed — like that of a BBC Radio 4 announcer. You are being asked to do that which you have been trained to do over five years — you are being asked to write in the style of the discursive essay.

Another aspect of the instructions to which I want to draw your attention is the statement that:

> *the essay should contain your view, taking into account the points made in these items.*

That the essay should contain your view is in no way an invitation for you to present whatever view you like; this is not carte blanche for you to indulge your personal predilections. You must base that view *entirely* on the material presented to you:

> *you must base your conclusion entirely on the material presented to you, and on any direct inferences you can draw from it.*

Following this first paragraph of instructions, you will be given a list of the items or documents which will constitute the material to be used by you. Read this list carefully and do not ignore any of the items in it. Every item is there to help you, and if you omit or ignore one then you can land yourself in trouble. For example, some candidates in the 1990 examination ignored the map (see Appendix) with the result that they confused the locations of Aonach Mor and Lurcher's Gully: some thought that they were one and the same site, others thought that they were very near to each other. For them it was downhill all the way!

Look carefully, then, at the list of items and make sure that you omit none in your deliberations.

Next, you must read off the items in turn, studying each one in detail. Once you have read them all, then you will have some idea of what the *issue* is — you will see that there is, emerging from your study of all the material, a conflicting argument. The more you examine the material, the more your own viewpoint will emerge: and that is what is meant by the statement that "the essay should convey your own view". In the 1990 paper, for example, there are two possible viewpoints: either you support the conservationists or you support the developers of ski facilities, though a careful reading of the material should persuade you that the task of writing the essay is that bit easier if you support the conservationists and draw on the evidence given about Lurcher's Gully. Having said that, I have to stress, however, that I am only pointing out that to support the conservationists makes the task a little bit easier; it does not make you right! There is no right or wrong viewpoint. What you are judged on is your ability to present the arguments.

The problem was that many candidates ignored the points about Lurcher's Gully, consequently ignoring most of the conservationists' arguments, thus presenting a report which lacked evaluation and balance: such candidates did not do well.

One point must be made very clear, however: since you are writing for people "who might have a general interest in the argument", you have to present both sides of the argument, while, of course, agreeing with one of them. In other words, however much you disagree with one side of the argument, you cannot ignore it. You have to deal with it — and deal with it using the material you have been given! You cannot simply make up arguments of your own to demolish those points of view with which you disagree. If you take the 1990 paper, again as an example, you could not present the pro-skiing point of view and either ignore the conservationists' point of view or dismiss that point of view as just silly without losing marks. Those candidates who based their answers almost entirely on the Aonach Mor material were inclined to ignore the pro-conservation arguments, and consequently suffered in terms of marks.

Now that you have got to the stage of having digested the material and made up your mind on your viewpoint, you must go ahead and plan your essay. There are many ways of doing this, but I think the most effective is to go through the material again making notes or to mark on the paper itself those arguments for the point of view you support and those arguments against it.

Of course, I realise that you want to keep your exam paper for posterity, to impress your future grandchildren with your cleverness since your exam will inevitably have proved to be more intellectually demanding than the electronic multiple choice affair that they will key into their interactive little terminals — you can't call that sitting an exam! Of course, you must keep your paper, but that shouldn't stop you making little marks on it that will enable you to attain the highest grade — something that will impress not only your grandchildren but those relations a little closer in time. I suggest you mark those arguments that support your point of view with a wiggly line and those that oppose it with a solid line: it is quicker to underline than it is to make notes, and it makes it easier for you to refer back when you come to write the essay.

You have by this time a good grasp of what the material is about, a viewpoint, and arguments which support and oppose that viewpoint. All you have to do now is organise your answer. You see one of the things the examiners will be looking for is your ability to *evaluate* the given material. You have first of all to organise the points you have underlined into *related groups*. You may find, for example, that some of the issues are purely practical, while others may well be of a more philosophical or moral nature; some may be related to procedure, while others are more concerned with the substance or "content" of the procedure — much depends on the nature of the issue presented to you.

Once you have organised the arguments into related groups, you then have to evaluate the groups of arguments to assess which one most effectively supports your point of view. Then you have to sketch out your plan: decide what needs to go in to the introduction, remembering that the reader, though educated, is not an expert and will need to be introduced to your argument; then decide the points you want to make and how you will use each paragraph to make the points; finally, you outline the conclusion in which you will sum up the argument without introducing any new material.

By now, you are ready to start writing. You are probably wondering right now: "How much time have I left! He expects me to read the stuff several times, decide on a viewpoint, underline like mad — which means read it all again — and then do a plan! That will take me ages! I'll never get it written!" And, of course, you are quite right, it will take up a lot of time to go through all the procedures I suggest before you start writing. But I do not apologise.

Remember, you have quite a lot of time in the first place. It does say right at the beginning of the paper:

You should spend approximately one hour on this part of the paper.

An hour is quite a long time, especially if you know what you are doing. If you don't know what you are doing, the minutes can tick away deafeningly in thought-defying panic. There is always a great temptation in any exam, and in all parts of this exam, not to plan, but to get on with the job of writing. Resist it, or it will cost you dear. Begin by thinking things out and planning.

After all, you are going to write about 350 – 400 words — about two to three sides of your examination answer book. That should not take you any longer than 30 to 35 minutes, especially if you know what you are doing! You have then 25 minutes (or more) to spend on the activities I suggested above: 10 minutes to read the material thoroughly in the first instance, a couple of minutes to decide on your viewpoint, 10 to underline and group the arguments, and 5 to sketch out your plan. Actually, you don't even need 30 minutes in which to write the essay; the more work you put in to the planning stage, the less time you need to spend writing it, but since you won't believe me, we'll leave it that you need about 35 minutes to do the writing.

The Introduction.

It never fails to amaze me that so very many candidates pay such scant regard to an introduction. You have to assume that your reader knows very little about the issue that is the subject matter of the report. He or she needs, then, to be put in the picture, to be given some kind of context for what is about to come. Use the introduction wisely to provide that context and to set out your views. Look at the way one candidate in 1990 introduced the skiing report:

> The development of skiing facilities will always prove to be a contentious issue. But nowhere is the debate more fierce than in Scotland, a land of unrivalled natural beauty. As any proponent of the developments will be sure to point out, however, there are clear advantages to be gained from them. They attract tourism and hence jobs to rural communities and they enable more people to share the joys of the Scottish winter landscape. But the impact of skiing on the environment, both visible and invisible, is permanent; it outlasts the propaganda battles and the wars of words.

Now there are tiny flaws, but you must agree that this introduction does its job: the reader is made clearly aware of the subject matter and the issues. And note how the writer does it: he begins with a general statement of the issue — "The development of skiing facilities will always prove to be a contentious issue" — and then goes on to give the issue its context which in this case is geographical. Finally, in this introduction, he explains the nature of the contentiousness.

Not every introduction need follow this formula, but all must do the job of making the subject matter and the issues clear for the reader.

The Development.

In this, the main section of your essay, you marshall all the arguments and present your case. Remember that there is no right or wrong answer, no right or wrong side to the argument; you decide your viewpoint and argue for that as best you can drawing all your support from the items you have been given. Go through the 1990 report (as I suggested previously) and group the points: pro-conservationist arguments and pro-skiing arguments. Once you have done that evaluate the arguments — which are the most important and which the least, given the point of view you have chosen to adopt?

Plan out your response to this the development stage of the report, the stage where you set out the arguments. After you have planned what it is you are going to say, then draft your essay, paying close attention to the mechanics of the language. Write accurately and precisely, and do not ignore formality: after all, you are being tested on your ability to write formal continuous prose.

Now compare what you have done to this response by one of the candidates in 1990. He scored 33 out of 35, which is, you'll agree, a very respectable mark, and one to which you should aspire! You have already read the first paragraph:

> The development of skiing facilities will always prove to be a contentious issue. But nowhere is the debate more fierce than in Scotland, a land of unrivalled natural beauty. As any proponent of the developments will be sure to point out, however, there are clear advantages to be gained from them. They attract tourism and hence jobs to rural communities and they enable more people to share the joys of the Scottish winter landscape. But the impact of skiing on the environment, both visible and invisible, is permanent; it outlasts the propaganda battles and the wars of words.

Those who support the new skiing developments in Scotland have a number of different reasons for doing so. Many argue that it can only be beneficial to give children and others the opportunity to share in the natural heritage. The main arguments used by those in favour of developments, however, are commercial. The Highlands and Islands Development Board, for example, argues that it is only right to capitalise on the natural resources of the Highlands. The Aonach Mor development, which has run into fierce opposition from conservationists, is an example of this. The planned complex, to include a car park, restaurant, shop and ski-hire facilities, as well as a chair-lift, will, it is argued, improve the area's job and tourism prospects. The skiing capacity of Scotland's slopes could, it is argued, be increased by half as much again if more developments, such as this one, were to go ahead.

The opponents of the developments are also well armed for the war of words which has ensued, however. The area of greatest controversy, in terms of environmental damage, is the proposed development at Lurcher's Gully in the Cairngorm mountains. The site has been designated a "site of scientific interest" and it is argued that the proposed development would, as well as being an eyesore, detrimentally affect the fragile ecosystem of the gully. The environmental lobby is relatively sizable, with well over a million supporters. So revulsion at the proposed developments, which could mean permanent and irreparable damage to areas of outstanding beauty, is by no means restricted to a minority.

The battles have been hard fought and they are by no means over yet. Tactics have often been devious on both sides, but this only shows how strongly each side feels about the matter. While it is essential that our rural communities should continue to survive and while it is essential that as many as possible are allowed to share in our natural heritage, we must all think of the future. We must exercise reason in all decisions pertaining to the environment. It is necessary to remember that, whilst our pleasure and economic welfare must not go unnoticed, we must ensure that our country survives unscarred for the coming generations to enjoy. (470 words)

You may exclaim: 33 out of 35 — why not 35/35! It may seem a bit mean not to give this essay full marks because it is really very good indeed. My main criticism of it is that it tends to lack bite. Part of the problem is that there are too many instances of "it is argued that" and "it is necessary" and "it is essential". It is written in what the writer thinks of as formal English and what I think of as committee English! You know the style: "The Committee feels that there are too many hooligans on the teaching staff." In English you can choose to write in what is called the Active Voice or in the Passive Voice. You don't really need to know these terms, but they are best explained by means of an example:

The girl hits the boy

is a sentence written in the *active voice* — the grammatical subject, "The girl", is the same as the doer of the action, whereas —

> *The boy was hit by the girl*

is written in the *passive voice* — the grammatical subject, "The boy", is not the same as the person who performs the action. Now there are a number of people who feel that formal English means that everything should be written in the passive voice: I hasten to assure you that this is not the case. In fact, I feel that the overuse of the passive creates the kind of deathly prose enjoyed by only the most wearisome of readers.

There is another myth fogging up the thinking of the country: that you must never use the first person singular — "I" — in the formal essay. Let me at once dispel this myth. If it makes more sense to you, as the writer, to use the first person singular, then go ahead and use it. After all, the question asks you to express your viewpoint and it can often seem contrived to express your own views in the third person!

We have digressed a bit from the essay quoted on the previous page. As I said, it lacks bite, and I think that that is because so many of the sentence structures are passive.

The other thing to note about this essay is its length: 470 words. If you look at the instructions you will note that it says:

> You are unlikely to be able to complete this task in fewer than 350 words.

Nothing could be more certain. Whatever else you want to worry about when it comes to this question, do not worry about length. Too many candidates waste precious time counting their words. Don't! You need all your time to complete the task in an hour. The candidate whose essay is reproduced above took 470 words, and I think that every one of them is necessary.

The Conclusion.

I said much earlier that an effective conclusion can only enhance your essay, and that is true. Again, the above essay has a good conclusion which very neatly and concisely rounds off the argument. The reader is not left with the feeling that the essay has just been abandoned, and I'm afraid that too many essays leave markers with that impression. The writer of the above essay ends on the same kind of general note with which he began his piece, and that is good. He finishes by reminding us subtly of the issues (or contentions, as he calls them), while making clear his own viewpoint, and all that is achieved by his last sentence.

This has been a long chapter, but an important one, and one which, if you spend the time digesting all that it says, will nourish and replenish you for the great day itself. The report (or formal essay) is worth as many as 35 marks, therefore it is well worth paying it every attention. In any case, since this is a form of the discursive essay, and since discursive writing pervades every corner of this examination, then you neglect the skills it demands at your peril.

Chapter VI

CRITICAL ESSAY

Let me remind you again what Revised Arrangements say about the Critical Essay:

> Candidates will be required to write a critical essay of approximately 500 words in continuous formal prose on *one* of a choice of topics.
>
> There will be a number of literary topics arranged in three sections: Section A — Drama; Section B — Prose; Section C — Poetry. At least one question will always be concerned with Shakespearean drama. Works in translation, where appropriate, may be used. There will also be a number of topics relating to the mass media in a further section — Section D. The mass media topics will deal with each of the specified areas of study as well as offering more general questions.
>
> In all four sections it will be possible for a candidate to choose a Scottish text or texts as the basis for an answer.
>
> The specified areas of study of the mass media for 1991 will be:
>
>   Film;   Narrative;   Representations.
>
> In the first instance these areas of study will be set for a period of not less than three years. Thereafter, one or more than one of the specified areas will be changed, with one year's notice of change being given.

Right away you will notice the injunction to write in continuous formal prose; sadly a sizeable minority of candidates ignore this demand of the critical essay and suffer accordingly.

Exclusions

It is very important for you to realise that you are not completely free to use any text or even any genre you like in the Critical Essay. You should refer to Appendix 2 where the rules of the examination are set out for handy reference. I'll explain why, but perhaps this is the best place to explain the exclusions that operate in this Higher. As I said in Chapter I, whatever text is central to your RPR may not be used elsewhere in the examination. For example, if your RPR is an analysis of, say, aspects of the setting in *Wuthering Heights*, then you are prohibited from choosing the Specified Text question on that novel, nor are you allowed to use *Wuthering Heights* in the Critical Essay. That exclusion should be clear enough. Things, however, get a little more complicated.

If, in Paper I, you answer the Specified Text question on, say, *Death of a Salesman*, then you may not attempt the Drama Section in Paper II. In other words, if you choose to answer on a play in the Specified Text section of Paper I, then you cannot choose from the Drama Section of Paper II; similarly, if you choose to answer on a novel in the Specified Text section of Paper I, then you cannot answer from the Prose Section of Paper II; and so on for poetry.

You may, however, answer the Practical Criticism question (Paper I, Part 2, Section A) even if the passage there coincides with your choice for the RPR; moreover, if you choose the PC, then you are not excluded from answering the drama, prose or poetry sections in Paper II.

The only reason that might exclude you from the Mass Media Section in Paper II is if a radio, television or film script is the basis of your study in your Review of Personal Reading. Clear enough?

These exclusions are there, by the way, to try to ensure that you read as widely as possible: you cannot get through the examination solely on a diet of poetry, for instance. Because they are there and because you are told of them prior to your study for the examination, you can very effectively plan your course. You choose a text for the RPR knowing that you cannot then use that same text on the day of the examination. You can choose ahead of time (in fact, you'd be daft not to) which Specified Text you are likely to attempt in Paper I in the knowledge that you then cannot choose from the same genre as that text in Paper II.

And remember I said not to study more than two Specified Texts? The reason for that should be obvious enough: if you study one play, one poem and one novel for the Specified Texts, and on the day of the examination you answer the Specified Text question using, say, the novel, then you are almost bound to use either the play or the poem in the Critical Essay. And so determined are you in the Critical Essay to get in all those details of the text so carefully learned from the teacher and your notes that you forget completely what it is the question is actually asking: you are seduced into massive irrelevance. The examiners have seen it time after time after time.

My advice is threefold:

(a) study no more than two Specified Texts;

(b) keep an open mind about the PC as an option;

(c) don't use your other Specified Text in the Critical Essay.

I have already dealt with *(a)* in great detail. My advice in *(b)* is based on experience of performance in the examination. Only 14% of you will tackle the PC on the day of the examination, and that is a pity. So few of you choose to attempt PC, I suspect, because your teachers tell you not to: but my advice to you is that if you have studied literature using the method I recommended in Chapter I, then you are already well versed in the art of Practical Criticism.

Don't write off the PC. There is evidence that the abler candidate can in fact do very well in this question.

By *(c)* I mean that if you prepare two Specified Texts and you do one of them in Paper I, then do not use the other in Paper II. As I said above, there is a great deal of evidence that candidates who use a Specified Text in their Critical Essay are too easily tempted into irrelevance — the cardinal sin of this part of the paper.

The three genres of literature form three of the sections in this paper: Drama, Prose, and Poetry. The fourth section is Mass Media. You have to answer one question only, though your choice, as I have explained at length, will be circumscribed if you have answered a Specified Text question in Paper I. That still means that you have plenty of choice.

That you have so much choice and that you have to answer only one question in fifty minutes is borne in mind by the setters of this part of the paper. You will see that questions are a little more specific, a little less open-ended, than you might otherwise have expected.

Think for a moment about the genre we call prose: there is the novel, the twentieth century novel, the pre-twentieth century novel, the short story, the biography and autobiography, the travel book, the essay, journalism. And there are only four questions. The brightest among you will have already worked out that since four questions cannot cover a list that long, some items on the list will be left out from time to time. The setters cannot leave out the novel (if they did, the outcry would drown the wind and make mad a whole horde of people), but you can see yourself that they cannot guarantee to set a question that would suit the one novel you have studied. Therefore study more than one novel, and don't forget the other items on the list: you cannot be assured of a question on the short story, but if you have studied a pre-twentieth and a twentieth century novel, two or three essays, and some journalism as well, then all your options are bound to be covered.

It is the same with poetry. To go in to this exam having studied only a couple of poems is to flirt with disaster. During your preparation for the exam you'll decide on what it is you are going to do on the day of the examination. You know that you are going to look at the PC, but you also know that you are more than likely going to tackle *Death of a Salesman* as long as the questions suit you. That means that ahead of time, during the preparation stage, you know that you will be unlikely to do drama; you can then concentrate your study on prose and poetry. You know that this is how you are going to prepare for the examination, but your examiners know it as well.

That is why they make the questions that little bit more challenging and why choice is more restricted than you might hope for: they know you are likely to be preparing for only two sections, and they are setting the exam to make sure that you cannot get away with the minimum of work for those two sections! If you are only going to study for two sections, then make sure you study fairly extensively within your chosen genre.

So, study more than a couple of poems. Like prose, poetry divides into a number of sub-genres: narrative, lyric, dramatic monologue, humorous, sonnet, epic; and it also divides into periods such as the Romantic, the Augustan, the Metaphysical. I can refer you to *The Practical Guide to Poetry* (Robert Gibson & Sons, 1990) for further explanation. When I say that you should study more than a couple of poems, I do mean from more than one sub-genre. Three poems by one author would still be too thin a diet; you need to add to that repertoire different kinds of poems by other authors, preferably from eras other than our own.

I am stressing that the ideal course for this examination is not only a wide-ranging one, but one which involves you in a little depth of study as well. Those who believe that they can get through this examination on a minimum of texts will find their faith broken by the results.

The study of literature is important, not because you have to sit an exam next May, but because literature develops us as people. Our reading affects the way in which we write, and as we become aware of our own techniques as authors, we learn a critical awareness of such techniques in others. English, as I have said many times elsewhere, is not made up of separate, discrete skills: each skill we master as students of English helps us to master all.

This is not the paper for prescribed texts, only proscribed ones, though the proscription is determined by your own choice elsewhere. There will, however, always be an opportunity to write on a Shakespearean text.

The Critical Essay is, sadly, very badly done. The main problem is one of irrelevance: too many candidates are too reluctant to pay any attention to the question. Let's put it more positively: it is vitally important in this paper to answer the question that actually has been asked. Candidates are only too ready to write down all they know about the text, or, more accurately, all that they have been told about the text, as though they hadn't seen the question. It is as though they are exploding all they know on the page on the hope that some of it will hit the target. Here you are, Mr. Examiner, here's all I know, now you sort it out, you work out which bits answer that silly question and which bits don't.

That approach simply will not do. It's your job to sort out from your knowledge what is relevant and what isn't in terms of the question asked, and it is your job to do that because the assessment of your ability to answer relevantly is part of the purpose of the examination. The examination sets out to measure your ability to select relevantly from your knowledge and to pursue the line of argument suggested by the question.

The Approach to the Critical Essay

What, then, you may ask, is the best approach to this part of the paper?

First of all you must not forget the importance of studying a range of texts — and remember what I have said about not using your other specified text. The PC is going to be an option worthy of your most serious consideration, therefore you need to prepare for at least three sections of this paper. Even if you decide to do the Specified Text section of Paper I, there is no harm in having prepared for three sections, though of course you will remember that you cannot attempt the same genre as that specified text in Paper II. What is a reasonable range of texts? In a sense I cannot answer that since so much depends on the amount of work you have to commit to your other subjects. Nevertheless, I would say that you should know at least two plays, two novels (or one novel and some short stories), some non-fiction, and more than four poems by more than two poets. If you are preparing a specified text then that should be in addition to all of these. Ideally, of course, you should do more than what I am suggesting; success in Higher English, and by "success" I mean gaining a "B" award or above, comes from having read widely and in depth.

Then, you have to set about studying and coming to terms with your chosen texts. The work for the Critical Essay obviously cannot be done overnight; it has to be done as you study the text in class, using your time at home to read, re-read, reflect and respond. When it comes to studying any work of literature, film, television play, soap opera, whatever, bear in mind the three questions:

 (a)   What is the novel/play/poem about?
   (Getting to know the text.)

 (b)   What are the effects on me?
   (How do I react — cry, laugh, feel sad, bored?)

 (c)   How have these effects been produced?
   (What techniques has the author used to bring about this reaction in me?)

You have to reflect on what *you* think are the issues or themes raised by the text, and your answers to question *(a)* will help you work these out. It is important that *you* work out the themes and issues for yourself, rather than depend on notes to make up your mind for you, since an important demand of this Higher is that you demonstrate *your personal* response to the text and your engagement with it. I'll explain that further.

I hope I made it very clear in Chapter I that in your RPR you have to show your involvement in the text; you have to be able to demonstrate that you are *not* regurgitating what someone else has said about the text you have chosen, but that you yourself have ideas about this text. After all, *you* chose it, and that choice must indicate that you are interested in it: show that interest, show that the text affects you. Read again the RPR I quoted, because it does all that.

The same kind of response is required in the Critical Essay, even although it is written under exam conditions. If, in your answer to one of the critical essay options, you simply stick down everything you know, especially if all that you know is based on notes, either your teacher's or some publisher's, then there is little chance that you are demonstrating your own interest in and engagement with the text. Bear in mind that able candidates don't need notes and the less able can't use them. In any case, in order to pass, that is, in order to get a "C" award, you have to show *some* personal involvement. And that doesn't mean that you tag on a last sentence that says, "Oh, by the way, I fairly enjoyed *The Suicide* by Louis MacNeice". What you have to show isn't necessarily your enjoyment — only the stupid or the perverse could claim to "enjoy" a poem about such an event — but your involvement; that somehow the text said something to you, it related to some aspect of your imagination or experience, and you have to show that, not state it.

If you have prepared for the examination by using the questions I have suggested here and elsewhere, then you have little to worry about. "What are the effects on me?" answered honestly and thoughtfully will provide you with the right kind of notes — your own notes — which you can go over the night before the exam. Of course you need to go that stage further and answer the next question, "How have these effects been created?", since your responses to that question will provide you with the meat for the exam itself.

Let's now assume that you have done all the necessary preparation and you are thoroughly acquainted with all your chosen texts. The next problem is how to go about answering the question in the Critical Essay section. To begin with you have to remember that you have to do only *one question* and that you have about *fifty* minutes in which to do it. That may sound wonderful — if anything to do with an examination could ever be said to be wonderful, but you know what I mean — that may sound wonderful, but you have to be careful: because you have to answer only one question and because you have fifty minutes in which to answer it, a bit more is expected than just three sides of examination paper. You are expected to be able to produce a thoughtful, relevant, structured, formal response which will demonstrate your knowledge and understanding of the ideas of the text of your choice, as well as your personal involvement in it.

How do you set about producing a top answer? To achieve such an academic perfection, the glittering prizes, and the consequent parental accolade, you need to know what you are doing.

Firstly and basically, you need to have done the work at home. (As I said in the Introduction, I often think that *work* is really the meanest, nastiest and most shocking of all the four letter words. There is no way of avoiding it — if there were, I would have marketed the technique and would be, by now, living luxuriously and shamelessly in the Bahamas on the profit. But, I fear, if you want to do well you must accept the inevitable and the unavoidable, and just get down to some honest labour with your books.)

You then need to know how to answer the question asked such that you can earn high marks. Here I can help you a little. We shall use a concrete example: a real question, with real advice about how to tackle it, followed by a real answer.

First the question:

> "— marriage and birth and death and thoughts of these —"
>
> Show how "thoughts of these" are evoked in you by a poem which deals with one or more of these themes. Explain by close reference to the techniques of the poem how the theme(s) is/are made memorable for you.

Now the advice. Note that in effect you have to do three things:

(a) you have to show how one or more than one of the themes mentioned are evoked in you by a poem you know;

(b) you have to refer closely to the techniques of the poem; and

(c) by reference to these techniques, you have to show how those themes are made memorable for you.

Right away you should notice the number of references to you yourself. The question demands a personal response: you have to deal with how the themes are evoked in you, and how they are made memorable for you. If you fail to involve yourself in your answer to this question, you will be unlikely to gain more than a minimum pass — at best.

You are aware of the question, you've had the advice, what next? Well, next comes the *plan*. I know that, whatever I say here, you will very largely ignore it. You are frightened to "waste time" producing a plan, but believe me time spent in planning is not time wasted. Remember that the cardinal sin in this part of the paper is irrelevance, and a plan will help you avoid committing that particular sin. You have, after all, about 50 minutes in which to answer the question. You need to write about 500 words, and since it does not take more than 30 minutes to write that number of words, that leaves you 25 minutes in which to plan. I know and you know that you will never ever risk spending 25 minutes planning an answer, but even if you devote 10 – 15 minutes to that occupation, then you will reap the benefits.

What about the plan for this question? Very often the question itself will provide you with a structure or outline for a plan. Such is the case with this particular question: you really need to deal with how the themes are evoked in you by the poem and then go on to deal with how the techniques used by the poet help those themes become memorable for you. You must also remember, as always, *to make close reference to the text* in order to support any claims you are making.

Your essay must begin with an introduction, and the points you want to make should be included therein. After all, that is what an introduction is for: to introduce the reader to what you are about to say, provide a context for the reader so that he or she can the more readily understand your meaning.

The introduction, then, should open with the words of the question and should set out the structure of your essay. Thereafter, each paragraph which follows should contain each of the points set out in the introduction. In each paragraph you also should refer back to the question, and you should refer closely to the text you are using as the basis for your answer. By referring back to the question in each paragraph, you will help to keep yourself relevant and prevent yourself from being seduced into soggy narrative. There's nothing worse. And by referring closely to the text, you are demonstrating to the examiner your knowledge of the text and your ability to select relevantly from that knowledge to support the points you are making.

Your answer should really be in the form of an argument. The question sets you a task and suggests a line of argument: your job is to fulfil that task by presenting a line of argument. Of course, and I stress this, you do not need to support that line of argument, you are free to refute it, but in so doing you have to be able to present the counter-argument.

Doesn't it all sound vaguely familiar? It most certainly should, since this is the very way I suggested you should proceed with your RPR. The skills are really the same, the only difference being that in the RPR you set your own task and produce your own line of argument, whereas here the task is set for you. All this means, in effect, that the skills you gain and practise in tackling your RPR will stand you in good stead here in the Critical Essay.

Let's recap: you have your introduction planned and you know the points you want to make in each of the ensuing paragraphs. And you are remembering that you have to refer back to the question and to the text itself. All that remains is the conclusion, the function of which, as always, is to draw together all that you have been saying, to leave the examiner with the best possible impression of your knowledge and your writing skills, and to round off neatly, economically, and concisely the argument. It is most assuredly not the place to be introducing anything new.

Once again, I am going to present you with an answer that was produced under examination conditions. And, once again, it isn't perfect, but that is perhaps all to the good since its lack of perfection probably means that it is within your reach.

The following essay scored 28 out of 30 marks. I think I should point out that the candidate had made an extensive plan, and that most certainly was to his good. The candidate is answering the question on page 82.

In Philip Larkin's poem "Church Going", thoughts of "— marriage and birth and death . . ." are evoked through a progression of thought, change and mood in the person of the narrator. He moves from a trivial everyday event, visiting a church, to a universal statement on mankind's conditions of which those in the title of this question are central.

The theme of the poem, which is a confirmation of the importance of the central events in human life and the church — marriage and birth and death — is similarly made memorable by this progression of thought.

The narrator is someone visiting a church, possibly Larkin himself. When this person first enters the church it is only "Once I am sure there's nothing going on". He does not want to be present at a service and thus immediately his attitude appears to the reader as one of flippant scepticism. The visitor then has a look around the inside of the church. He sees "matting, seats, and stone, / And little books". However, it is just a list, said without any feeling. This shows the visitor's apparent detachment from the church, and his use of "little books" seems actually to belittle them. He continues to look around the church and uses pejorative words, such as "stuff" and "holy end". "Stuff" is one of those indeterminate words, indicating that he does not know what any of the things are, and "holy end" seems almost to liken the altar to a football ground. All of this creates the feeling of bored ignorance on the visitor's behalf. The visitor does note, however, the presence of "a tense, musty, unignorable silence" which shows that he does perhaps feel something of interest or importance in this place after all.

In his state of apparent boredom, the visitor then looks up at the roof of the church for something to do. He says:

> From where I stand, the roof looks almost new —
> Cleaned or restored? Someone would know: I don't.

Again the visitor seems to have little real interest. He then mounts the lectern and looks at the scriptures. He calls them "Hectoring large scale verses", again a phrase that is derogatory in tone. He reads aloud and the echoes "snigger" briefly, though it is really the poet's attitude that is sniggering, a thought which is confirmed by the flippancy of the fact that he donates an Irish sixpence.

At this stage the visitor prepares to leave, reflecting that "the place was not worth stopping for". However, he does stop: "Yet stop I did: in fact I often do, / And always end much at a loss like this". This change of attitude from snide cynicism has been prepared for by the "Unignorable silence" and the earlier "awkward reverence". The visitor's attitude has now changed to a more serious one. He is not as "uninformed" as he would like us to think. He knows terms such as "plate and pyx", and the use of the word "chronically", more often applied to a serious illness, seems to confirm this change. He uses phrases such as "pick simples for a cancer" and "on some / Advised night see walking a dead one" all of which have archaic undertones, further suggesting the author's changed attitude.

There is a darkening of the mood when the visitor contemplates those who will visit an old, decayed church just to see a ruin. His use of the word "crew" suggests that the visitor regards such people with contempt, and words such as "ruin-bibber", "randy" and "addict" all create a feeling of anger.

The visitor then goes on to offer a solution to the problem he has posed himself: why did he stop and enter the church? He says that the church is a confirmation of the importance of the central events in human life. The church has:

> held unspilt
> So long and equably what since is found
> Only in separation: marriage, and birth,
> And death, and thoughts of these . . .

The church acts as a unifying force for all three of these eternal events and its importance is derived from this fact.

The visitor's new and deeper feelings, as a result of the recognition of the church's importance, are shown in a number of ways. In the last stanzas the word "serious" is repeated three times. Various dignified terms are used, such as "gravitating", "robed", and "destinies". The last stanza of the poem consists nearly entirely of single-line statements. The use of alliteration: "recognised and robed" and "gravitating to this ground", as well as the steady rhythm, mean that this last stanza is said slowly and with dignity.

Thus, through the visitor's progression of thought, tone, and attitude, as explained in this essay, he moves from cynicism to a universal statement on the value of the church. Its value is derived from its ability to unify marriage and birth and death, and thus the change in tone and mood evokes the "thoughts of these". The change from flippant scepticism to serious evaluation, also shown through changes in mood and tone, succeed in making the theme of this poem, the importance of the central events in human existence and of the church and its place in society, extremely memorable to the reader.

This candidate has written 880 words, considerably more than is really expected. I think you will agree, though, that it really is a very good piece of work. You might well wonder why it didn't attract full marks; the reason is simple: it lacks the enthusiasm and perceptive insight that we would associate with 30 out of 30. Nevertheless, it is excellent and it did get very high marks indeed.

You will no doubt have noted that it follows the pattern I suggested. There is a very good introduction which makes clear to the reader the candidate's grasp of the issue. The ensuing paragraphs take up the points as he wants to make them, and each point made demonstrates his knowledge and understanding, not only of the poem itself, but also of the task he has been set. When he wants to support his argument, there is accurate and unforced reference to the text. By "unforced" I mean that the quotations are neatly worked in to what he is saying and don't appear to be tagged on in order to prove that he has learned them.

There is also one of the best conclusions I think I have ever seen in Higher English: it is neat, concise, and to the point. It not only rounds off his argument, but makes reference to the opening paragraph, which gives his essay a "planned" feel. And, in fact, it was planned, which is why he is so able to come back to his opening paragraph in his concluding one. Very cleverly done.

There is also in this essay a very strong personal response. It isn't stated obviously, but it is implied by the very nature of his intellectual grasp of what the poem is about.

My only criticism is that he tends to be a bit imprecise when he comes to discuss language features: he sees that there is alliteration, and he can refer to it, but he cannot make fully clear how that alliteration, and the steady rhythm for that matter, do slow the stanza down. Another example is when he is discussing the word "crew": he seems to get the wrong idea of the word, the wrong connotative area, because what he says doesn't fit the meaning, nor does he even attempt to tell us how "ruin-bibber", "randy", and "addict" create the feeling of anger. If you read that verse of the poem for yourselves you will see what I mean. His interpretation seems a little bizarre, which is fair enough, but he fails to demonstrate how he arrives at that interpretation, which is a weakness in his answer.

Nevertheless, this is the kind of response you want to aim at, and if you follow all that I have said, *and put it into practice*, then you should be successful.

Whatever else, remember that in this question the two keys to some of that success are:

(a) answer the question asked *relevantly*; and

(b) give a lively and personal response.

Both tend to be forgotten with perilous results. You *must* be relevant and you *must* demonstrate your personal involvement in the text you have chosen to write about.

Conclusion

The best way to prepare for this, or any other examination in English, is to read widely, intelligently, and critically, paying close attention to the ways in which the author creates his or her effects. You should read quality newspapers (of which there are a surprising number nowadays), travel books, autobiographies, biographies and, of course, fiction. But read in low gear, being aware of the effects and how they are being created.

This book is intended to be a practical guide to the examination itself; it needs to be read in conjunction with the companion books: *The Practical Guide to*

Higher Literature and *The Practical Guide to Poetry*, both published by Robert Gibson & Sons. Success on the day of the examination depends not only on your having followed the advice within these pages (and within the pages of those books), but also on the extent and quality of your reading.

The exam tests only a sample of the skills acquired by you on the Higher Grade Course. On the day of the exam, then, don't be thrown by anything unusual.

A few final words: remember that this exam tests more than any other exam your skills in discursive writing. But also remember the importance of a personal response to your chosen texts, a personal response which is securely supported by plenty of close references to those texts.

Literature isn't written with the sole purpose of ensuring that you will spend your precious time preparing for tedious examinations and that old(ish) people like me will spend our even more precious time (we have less of it) in marking them. Literature is there to be read and enjoyed for its own sake. And it is my fervent hope that, long after you have forgotten Higher English and all the pain that went into the study for it, you will read a novel, or a poem, or you will visit the theatre, simply because you want to, because there is something in the text or in the performance that has something special and unique to say to you. That is what literature is really about.

APPENDIX 1 — 1990 PAPER II — Part 1

You should spend approximately one hour on this part of the paper.

Read the various items which follow, and then, when you have decided your own viewpoint, write an essay for people who might have a general interest in the argument. The essay should convey your view, taking into account the points made in these items. You must base your conclusion entirely on the material presented to you, and on any direct inferences you can draw from it.

On pages three and four, you have the following four groups of documents to help you. (The information at the foot of this page is simply to help you understand the situation.)

(i) *Three newspaper articles about the development of skiing facilities in Scotland*

(ii) *Three extracts from official documents concerned with the balance between conservation of the environment and commercial development*

(iii) *Two personal views expressed about ski development*

(iv) *Notes of an interview with an interested party*

Write your essay in formal continuous prose. The task involves reorganising the material, selecting relevant information, and presenting your conclusions. You are unlikely to be able to complete this task in fewer than 350 words.

NB Abbreviations used in the documents

HIDB = Highlands and Islands Development Board
NCC = Nature Conservancy Council
SSI = Site of Scientific Interest
SSSI = Site of Special Scientific Interest
RSPB = Royal Society for the Protection of Birds

MAP OF NORTHERN SCOTLAND SHOWING SKI DEVELOPMENTS

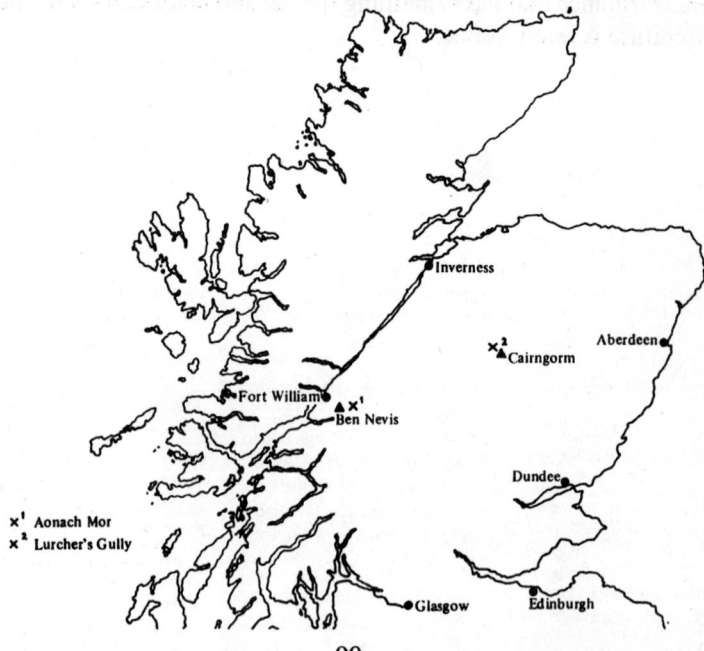

(i) **Newspaper articles**

Tourist Expansion

When so many major industrial enterprises have failed, the Highlands and Islands Development Board (HIDB) attaches great significance to developments which capitalise on the Highlands' natural resources and is keen to develop tourism into an all-year-round business. The multi-million pound development of skiing at Aonach Mor, near Ben Nevis, is expected to add to Fort William's summer trade. "The developers expect to do as well in summer as they will in winter, ferrying people up the mountain to admire the views," the Board spokesman said.

Conservationists view such incursions into the wilderness with alarm. "There is always going to be conflict," the Board spokesman admitted. "We have got to get people together to arrive at an acceptable solution."

New battle looms over Lurcher's Gully

A forecast of a second and much bloodier battle over Lurcher's Gully in the Cairngorms as the ski lobby puts forward new expansion plans has come from the Scottish Wild Land Group. The group claimed that the Cairngorm Chairlift Company, whose application was turned down after a public enquiry in 1981, was to submit a fresh application for development.

Early in 1988 a working group consisting of the Chairlift Company, local and national planning interests, and official conservationist bodies failed to agree on the future of skiing development in the Cairngorms.

The Scottish Wild Land Group says that the 1981 application was turned down because the conservation side had prepared a better case than the developers, but this time, although the conservation lobby was still well organised, the pro-development side was much better organised than in 1981 and had been lobbying vigorously.

But there was increased international pressure on the government to take care of the environment. Also the area around the gully had been designated as an SSSI (Site of Special Scientific Interest). Downhill skiing was the only recreation which demanded permanent, unsightly mechanical installations on the hill.

Uphill fight for a downhill ski centre

The history of the Aonach Mor project has been as long and tortuous as the ski runs the developers hope will turn their vision into a tourist centre attracting thousands more tourists to the area around Fort William.

The uphill struggle to develop Aonach Mor, a 3999 foot summit, began almost five years ago when a group of local business men came up with the idea of a big downhill skiing centre near Britain's highest peak, Ben Nevis. The development from the start has been seen by some in the local community, in both business and local authority sectors, as a method of improving the area's tourism and job prospects.

It would inject cash into the local economy through wages and the influx of extra tourists. Mr Ian Milton, one of the leading lights in the project from the start, said in support of the proposals: "If anyone can think of a more practical way of creating so many jobs in the middle of winter in Lochaber, then we would love to hear of it."

The development is backed by investment from Highland Region, Lochaber District, and the Highlands and Islands Development Board, as well as finance from the private sector.

The complex will include gondolas linking a car park at the bottom of the mountain to a restaurant, shop, and ski hire facilities at the top station together with a chairlift and ski tows in Snow Goose Gully.

(ii) **Extracts from official documents**

Countryside Planning Yearbook 1984

Scottish planning guidelines for skiing

The Scottish Development Department issued a general strategy for Scottish skiing developments. The guidelines suggest that capacity could be increased by 50% through limited development at Cairngorm (though not Lurcher's Gully), Glenshee, and Glencoe, with new developments at Drumochter, Ben Wyvis and Aonach Mor. The NCC welcomed the report but the HIDB and the Scottish Tourist Board did not.

International Yearbook of Rural Planning 1987

"Everywhere, increasing use is leading to deterioration, and the growth of skiing related damage is noteworthy, especially in Cairngorm (though not Lurcher's Gully), Scotland."

Countryside Commission for Scotland

Protecting fine scenery does not mean fossilising the landscape. The appearance of the countryside is always changing in response to different patterns of land use. But man's thoughtless or ill-conceived activity can cause permanent scars, and lasting damage to exceptional views. The Commission has been developing the idea of a landscape strategy to ensure that the natural and man-made beauty of Scotland is protected against undesirable change and enhanced where necessary, as part of the national heritage.

(iii) **Personal views**

Cairngorm Crisis

My walk brought me through to a perfect view of the Northern Corries of Cairngorm, including Lurcher's Gully. Corrie Cas and Corrie na Ciste have been intensively developed for downhill skiing. This highly commercial sport undoubtedly brings much revenue to the area but its effect on the environment is severe, especially in terms of erosion, and the visual impact of ski tows, pylons and other infrastructure cannot be hidden. And there is now, for the second time in eight years, a proposal to extend the development west of Lurcher's Gully.

To me, and to countless others, the Cairngorms are very special. I find the whole area deeply inspiring and spiritually uplifting. It is wild land *par excellence* and any damage to it cuts like a knife through my soul.

The merits of development cannot be judged on simple economic terms; we have a moral duty to care for such places, to ensure that future generations can get to know and love them as we do. Unfortunately, those appointed to exercise such guardianship are not often up to the task.

The Lurcher's Gully development will be opposed by the NCC [Nature Conservancy Council] and by many recreation and conservation bodies. The total membership of these bodies is well over a million people. One thing which would help these people would be the opposition to the scheme by the Countryside Commission for Scotland. They are greatly concerned about finding a "balance" between conservation and development, but with skiing developments at Aonach Mor and Drumochter set to go ahead, I believe they have only one choice here. They must act to save the Northern Corries from despoliation.

A Message from the Mountains

The skiing slopes on Cairngorm are packed. More and more fences have been erected to provide more runs. The hill is a scene of total activity. It is hoaching with life.

But Aviemore is no longer equipped to meet the requirements of the Scottish skier. Proposals which have been put forward for an extension into Lurcher's Gully have met strong opposition.

I freely admit to being prejudiced. I want to see my compatriots make the fullest use of their own country. I also admit to a fury at some of the arguments used against the extension of the use of the hills. When someone makes a case that any part of Scotland should be preserved as "one of the last wilderness areas of Europe", my birse rises and I have to challenge the argument. By what right does anyone decree that I or any of my family must live in a wilderness?

I welcome any expansion of the skiing facilities in the Cairngorms. I relish every sight of children and others finding a new window on the world in the snows of the Cairngorms.

(iv) **Notes on the Aonach Mor development at Fort William**

The scheme backed by Lochaber District Council, Highland Regional Council, and the Highlands and Islands Development Board. The RSPB also approved.
Opposed by Nature Conservancy Council.
As soon as plan was suggested 3 sites on the mountain were declared SSIs.
BUT no really rare plants or birds in the area—simply that the whole area is scientifically of general interest.
In any case the mountain is already riddled with pipes for the Alcan aluminium factory at Kinlochleven.
Planning conditions set for the development are VERY stringent.
An Environmental Audit has been done of the mountain, noting the present state of erosion, etc. Any deterioration will have to be rectified by the developers.
Scotland as a whole is short of 300,000 ski days.
AND even if ALL the developments which at present have a green light—Aonach Mor, Ben Wyvis, Drumochter—do proceed, it still won't keep pace with demand. Aonach can only provide a possible 100,000 ski days when under way.
The success of the venture so far is probably because of:
    (1) local support
    (2) the developers themselves being mountaineers and skiers and so
    (3) talking the same language as the various lobbies represented.
Very difficult to reach compromise with the true conservationist. Seems that they reckon if they oppose everything 100% all the time and everywhere, they might sometimes manage to stop some developments.

APPENDIX 2

RULES OF THE EXAMINATION

This examination, as has been mentioned in various places throughout this book, has three important rules, which, if broken, could lead to such penalties being imposed that you don't accumulate enough marks to pass. It is important, then, that you know these rules and do not break them.

The first of these rules is easy to remember:

> *(a)* Whatever text you use as the basis of your Review of Personal Reading, then that book must not be used again anywhere else in the examination.

In other words, if your RPR is based on, say, *Sunset Song*, then you cannot answer the Specified Text question on *Sunset Song*, nor could you use that novel as a basis for an answer in the Critical Essay.

The second rule also applies to the Review of Personal Reading:

> *(b)* If the basis of your RPR is a media text — i.e., a radio, television or film script, then you cannot answer a question from the Mass Media section of the Critical Essay.

If, however, your RPR is a comparison of, say, the film version of *Cal* with the novel *Cal*, then you are not restricted from answering from the Media Studies Section. The restriction applies only if the basis of the RPR is a script.

The next rule applies to Paper I, Part 2, Section B — The Specified Texts:

> *(c)* If you choose, say, a play in the Paper I, Part 2, Section B (the Specified Text Section), then you are excluded from answering from the Drama Section in Paper II, Part 2. If you choose a novel in Paper I (Specified Texts), then you cannot answer from the Prose Section in Paper II, Part 2, The same with poetry.

Put another way, you must ensure that in Paper II, Part 2, The Critical Essay, you must answer on *a genre different from* that dealt with in Paper I, Part 2, Section B (Specified Texts).

The only exclusion from all this is Practical Criticism: if you tackle PC, then no matter what genre it is, you can answer any question in the Critical Essay (Paper II, Part 2), nor are you prevented from answering PC if it happens to be the subject of your RPR — though that is unlikely.

These rules are really very straightforward once you get to know them.

NOTES

NOTES